WORK−LIFE
AGILITY

Johnathon Herrington

First published 2020 by Indie Experts
PO Box 1638, Carindale
Queensland 4152 Australia
indieexperts.com.au

Copyright © Johnathon Herrington 2020 – All rights reserved.

Apart from any fair dealing for the purposes of study, research or review, as permitted under the copyright act, no part of this book may be reproduced by any process without written permission of the author.

Every effort has been made to trace and acknowledge copyright material; should any infringement have occurred accidentally, the author tends his apologies. Product and other names used herein may be trademarks of their respective owners. The author disclaims any and all rights in those marks.

Book cover by Jesse Bogaert (www.bogaertdesign.com.au)
Edited by Libby Turner
Internal design by Indie Experts
Typeset in 12.5/18 pt Adobe Garamond Pro by Post Pre-press Group, Brisbane

A catalogue record for this book is available from the National Library of Australia

ISBN 978-0-6488564-0-5 (paperback)
ISBN 978-0-6488564-1-2 (epub)
ISBN 978-0-6488564-2-9 (kindle)

Disclaimer:
The content of this book is for informational purposes only and is not intended to diagnose, treat, cure, or prevent any condition or disease. You understand that this book is not intended as a substitute for consultation with a licensed practitioner. Please consult with your own physician or healthcare specialist regarding the suggestions and recommendations made in this book. The use of this book implies your acceptance of this disclaimer.

CONTENTS

INTRODUCTION TO WORK–LIFE AGILITY   1

CHAPTER 1: LIVING ON PURPOSE   7
CHAPTER 2: THE MINDSET THAT MAKES HABIT CHANGE EASIER   21
CHAPTER 3: EATING WELL FOR WORK–LIFE AGILITY   33
CHAPTER 4: PHYSICAL MOVEMENT FOR MENTAL PERFORMANCE   45
CHAPTER 5: RECOVERY AND RESILIENCE   63
CHAPTER 6: HEALTHY WORKING RELATIONSHIPS   93
CHAPTER 7: THE ANTIDOTE TO PROLONGED SITTING   105
CHAPTER 8: HEALTH CHECKS AT EVERY AGE   125

CONCLUSION   143
ACKNOWLEDGEMENTS   145
THE AUTHOR   146
DISCLAIMER   148

INTRODUCTION TO WORK–LIFE AGILITY

If you're struggling to have enough time and energy for everything in your life, you're not alone. Out of the 35 countries in the Organisation for Economic Co-operation and Development (OECD), Australia ranks way down at number 27 for work–life balance. Within Australia, research has shown people in managerial and professional roles are the most likely to have poor work–life outcomes, compared to other occupations.

Work–life 'balance' is unachievable

There was a time when leaving the office for the day meant leaving your work behind. Now, we carry almost our whole job in our back pockets. We're expected to stay available by phone, email and text in the evenings, on weekends and even on holidays. It means we have no true separation from work to recharge and relax.

Digital advances have also accelerated the pace of change at work. For example, we have faster and more reliable international communication, access to more data, and constant connection to our workplaces. The rate at which we adopt new technology and products is faster than it was just a decade ago. As everything else in the business world moves more quickly, we are expected to as well.

As a result, most of us have lives of overwhelming busyness. We find ourselves under the constant pressure of competing demands, always 'doing'. We cut back on sleep to fit everything in and view time off as an unnecessary luxury. Work appointments take priority over personal appointments. Added to that are the increased demands in our personal lives. More and more of us are now balancing paid work and caring responsibilities, and the tension shows.

The Australian Bureau of Statistics reports that 35% of Australian men feel 'always or often rushed or pressed for time'. Women are even busier, with 42% being always or often pressed for time. And when you ask those who provide care, an even larger proportion say they're stretched – 46% of men and 55% of women. Over time, a lack of balance means we're unable to perform at our best. The damage extends to our health, our relationships and our quality of life.

As a performance coach, I see first-hand the costs of constantly pushing ourselves to achieve more without assessing how sustainable it is. Many of my clients are successful senior managers who have gradually noticed physical or psychological health problems as these health issues interfered with their performance at work and their personal lives. It's often almost too late before they realise that without their health, they would have nothing.

Why work–life agility beats work–life balance

I believe the reason so many of us struggle with work–life balance is the concept itself is flawed. Why choose between 'work' and 'life'? I don't want to treat work and life as opposing forces. Work should be a satisfying, enriching part of our life, not something we do while we put our real 'life' on hold.

Let's also consider the concept of 'balance'. If a seesaw is balanced, it means that the weights on each side are equal, and not changing. For work–life balance, it means that at any given moment, we are giving the same time and energy to both 'work' and 'life', with equal demands on us from both sides of the see-saw. But, of course, this never happens! Life is dynamic. Perhaps tomorrow you'll have a public relations crisis and that sucks up your attention. Or your child is having a small operation, so they need your focus. If you aim for the elusive 'balance', you will always feel guilty for dropping the ball in either your work or your home life. Or, most likely, both.

It is impossible to keep these constantly changing demands frozen in balance. What we *can* do is develop the vitality to quickly and easily move our energies where they are needed, and back again. Developing wellbeing in any area of our life supports our wellbeing, energy and performance in other areas of our life, whether it's work, family, friends, study, hobbies, or community activities.

> Work-life agility is the ability to quickly and easily respond to multiple demands and achieve goals that matter in all areas of life. We accomplish this by prioritising health and vitality, and by cultivating sustainable high performance.

Is this book the right one for you?

Work–Life Agility is for executives and senior professionals who don't want to choose between their professional ambitions and quality of life.

Consider your lifestyle at present. Does this sound familiar? You long for more hours in the day but are starting to realise the costs of burning the candle at both ends. Your family grumbles about your poor work–life balance, and your doctor might too. At the same time, you love your work and want to continue performing at the highest levels, achieving even more than you already have. In addition, there's also constant background pressure to have a decent, secure income to pay the bills. You've probably tried to improve your wellbeing in the past but found the new habits too time-consuming or too difficult. Perhaps they were a poor fit for your busy career.

Does this look like what you'd like more of in your life?
- You're seeking more energy to achieve goals in all areas of life
- You want to be able to consistently perform at your best while improving your health

- You crave better alignment between what you do each day and what's most important to you
- You know you need greater health, fitness and vitality

In this book, I'll give you a taste of the key actions and mindsets you need to set yourself up for sustainable excellence and health. I'll share the most important, practical and evidence-based habits you need to:

- spend your working hours in alignment with your values and purpose
- reach your wellbeing goals more easily by adjusting your mindset
- have nutritious food on hand for greater energy
- reap the health and performance benefits of the right type of exercise
- recover faster with improved sleep quality
- avoid the health risks of prolonged sitting (while boosting your brain)

Although I focus on protecting your long-term health and quality of life, many of my recommendations have immediate benefits. You'll move, feel, look and function better now and into the future.

About me

I've worked in the health and wellbeing industry as a high-performance coach for the past 20 years. I've helped thousands of my clients shape their lives to create optimal health and fitness, vitality and sustainable high performance.

I started my journey in the Australian military, in an elite group of high-performing soldiers. I gained a deep understanding of what it takes to work in high-pressure situations where exceptional performance is vital. I came to appreciate that it's not only your actions in the moment, but your entire lifestyle that sets you up for success on the day.

On completion of my military service, I furthered my training in health and coaching and specialised in working with executives and senior professionals. I've accumulated a vast knowledge and experience in fitness, nutrition, motivational and mindset coaching, high-performing individuals and teams, and personal leadership.

I have a strong personal purpose to provide information, guidance and a supportive space to help people achieve their goals in our current high-pressure environment. Not just in the short-term, but to create the conditions for excellence and vitality for decades to come.

I believe that everyone has the solutions to greater wellbeing within them.

I have seen what works for busy, high-performing professionals in a range of leading organisations and now, I've packaged up the best of it into this book.

I sincerely hope you're able to apply some of these practical strategies to develop your own work–life agility for wellbeing and success.

CHAPTER 1: LIVING ON PURPOSE

Are you one of those fortunate people who wake up each day with a sense of purpose? If so, you're no doubt enjoying a high level of wellbeing and performance. Purpose is one of the most powerful motivators in life.

However, many of us have been too busy to clarify our own purpose lately. It's easy to lose sight of what matters when we're constantly responding to multiple competing pressures. If that's you, you're not alone.

What is purpose and why does it matter?

Having a strong sense of purpose means accomplishing something important to you while living in alignment with your values and using your favourite strengths and skills. When you have purpose in your work, it gets rid of the tension between 'work' and 'life'. Instead of being separate, work should be a vital and fulfilling part of life.

Alignment between your individual purpose and how you

actually spend your time is a powerful contributor to wellbeing. Living in conflict with what matters can be associated with stress, depression and poor health.

Interestingly, having a clear sense of purpose might also be good for your financial health. Research conducted over nine years and published in 2016 found that among the 7,000 participants, those with a higher sense of purpose had a higher income and net worth. They were also more likely to increase their income and net worth over the following years.

It makes sense that knowing your purpose changes your life. Deep down, we all have a fundamental drive to find meaning in your life. Happily, once you know what it is, your sense of purpose becomes much easier to fulfill.

Using your core values to make confident decisions

Let's start with your core values. Are you clear on what you most want in your own life? Do you use those values to guide your daily decisions? Living in alignment with your values becomes infinitely easier once you've spelt out what they are.

When you know what matters most, you have a roadmap to help you choose between competing priorities. For example, imagine a relative recently passed, leaving you $10,000. The instructions are for you enjoy it immediately. It's fantastic news because your house is in desperate need of fresh flooring. However, you're also keen to take the family skiing in New Zealand. Assuming you can't afford both, you can use your values to make it an easy decision. Someone who knows their top value is memorable time with family can confidently choose the holiday. Someone else who values hosting guests in an impressive home will invest the money in replacing their floors.

Checking in with your values also makes tough decisions easier to live with. For example, have you ever been tempted to go for a job that gives you more authority, but also a shocking commute time? If having more say in your work life is most important to you, you can use that value to put up with the travel, but what if managing your health and stress is a higher priority right now? Then keeping sight of your values lets you confidently turn down the promotion.

As well as helping with life's big questions, being clear on your values shows you where to invest your time on a *daily* basis. If increasing your wealth matters but being healthy matters more, you can easily justify paying a personal trainer and having healthy meals delivered. If finances are the priority, then you have clear direction to skip the outside help and find a more frugal way to nurture your health.

One more awesome thing about knowing your values is that you can *always* keep moving in their direction. Life brings inevitable setbacks and inevitably we fail to achieve certain goals. But you can keep taking steps in the direction that matters, if you know what it is.

There is no right or wrong way to prioritise your personal values. Your priorities can change as you move to a different life stage, or as the result of your experiences. For example, sometimes it takes a traumatic experience like a medical diagnosis or a relationship break-up to provide clarity. Research in post-traumatic stress has made way in recent decades for the exploration of post traumatic *growth*. This is the 'silver lining' in the form of personal development that can happen after terrible experiences. Researchers have found that the more a traumatic experience disrupts our core values, the more growth we experience. The difficult time forces us to review and adjust our values and priorities in life.

Having trouble identifying your top values? Imagine you've snuck into your own funeral. What would you hope to hear people saying about you? How would you like them to summarise the impact of your years here on earth? (I suspect that 'She really nailed Inbox Zero' or 'He always had a polished car' may not be on your wish list.)

What do you think it would be like to find your purpose, clarify your core values and be empowered to live them and find greater joy in life?

Achieving your wishes for the world

Imagine you had a magic wand. What would you change in the world? What would you most like to see on this planet? Here is a short list of 'wishes for the world' to get you thinking. I'm sure you have other favourite causes and passions too:
- Financial literacy for young people
- Access to technology in developing countries

- Reduced waste
- More successful small businesses
- Stronger neighbourhood communities
- Support for people with a disability
- Access to health care in the poorest communities
- Higher standards of customer service in Australia
- Reduced stigma around mental illness.

Now, consider how you're making a difference in your work right now. It might fit exactly with one of your magic wishes for the world. When your efforts at work are invested in something you care about, it gives you more energy and helps you manage stress.

Or maybe you might feel you're working against what you'd like to see. That's OK. Later on, you'll see there are four ways (at least) to handle misalignment between your purpose and your profession.

Leveraging your signature strengths

Your signature strengths are the best parts of your personality. Just as we all have weaknesses, we all have strengths. It's easy to focus too much on our weaknesses and forget to harness those positive attributes that make us who we are.

When you acknowledge your strengths, you can more easily achieve what matters to you. One of the many positives of a strengths-based approach is that you focus on achieving even more with the gifts you already have. It beats spending all your time and energy on weaknesses that you will probably always struggle with.

Maybe creativity is one of your strengths, for example. This means coming up with ideas that result in something worthwhile. You can make the most of it by thinking of new and different ways to complete your work tasks.

Or is zest a better fit? This means you approach life feeling activated, enthusiastic and full of energy. You can use it by approaching a difficult task with enthusiasm and energy.

To discover your own signature strengths take the free, confidential and research-backed Values in Action inventory at https://www.viacharacter.org. Set aside at least ten minutes to complete the survey. The website provides fantastic information on how to explore and apply your strengths.

Achieving flow with the skills you love to use

What are you good at doing that you also love to do?

We all experience those times when we have been in a state of flow or 'in the zone'. It's when we're fully immersed in our task. We look up and we're surprised to discover an hour has gone by in what seemed like a few minutes. How do we achieve this flow state? It's more likely when we're faced with a challenging task and a high degree of skill.

Think about when you're in the zone and what skills you're using at the time. Think about different types of skills, such as:

- Technical skills (statistical analysis, programming)
- Interpersonal skills (negotiating, collaborating)
- Management skills (delegating, problem-solving)
- Self-management skills (time management, stress management)
- Thinking skills (reviewing, planning)

The more time you can spend using your favourite skills, the better for your performance and wellbeing.

Defining your purpose

Please take some time to reflect and record your thoughts on each of the following, to guide you to toward greater alignment with your own purpose.

Your values. What do you want most in your life?

Tick each value as either Not important, Nice to have, or Vitally important.

Values	Not important	Nice to have	Vitally important
Adventure			
Authority			
Balance			

Values	Not important	Nice to have	Vitally important
Beauty			
Challenge			
Community			
Compassion			
Connection to nature			
Creative and performing arts			
Equality			
Freedom			
Friendships			
Fun			
Growth			
Health			
Influence			
Justice			
Knowledge			
Leadership			
Learning			
Love			
Pleasure			
Recognition			
Relaxation			
Responsibility			
Security			
Self-Respect			
Sense of accomplishment			
Social Connection			

Values	Not important	Nice to have	Vitally important
Spirituality			
Stability			
Status			
Travel			
Wealth			
Wisdom			
(Other:)			

Your wishes. What are the causes that matter to you? What do you most want to see on this planet?

Look at the values you ticked as most important and circle your top five values.

1	
2	
3	
4	
5	

Your signature strengths. How do you like to do things?

1	
2	
3	
4	
5	

Your skills. What are the top five skills or abilities you love to use?

1	
2	
3	

4	
5	

Now what?

Consider how you spend your time, both on and off the clock. Does it fit with your purpose – your values, wishes for the world, strengths and skills?

Option one: Your job fits well with your purpose

Let's say having time to take care of your health is vital, and your part-time job includes company-funded health coaching. Nice. Or perhaps you're a 'greenie' and your job is to educate business owners about how to reduce their carbon footprint. High five! One of your signature strengths is persistence, and a skill you love to use is following-up potential clients, which you do most days. You're set!

Option two: Your job is not aligned with your purpose, but you find a way to make it fit

There are dozens of ways you can achieve better alignment with your purpose, but they won't all be obvious at first. Speak to trusted colleagues, your supervisor or a coach for more creative ideas.

Perhaps you'd like to see financial literacy improve, so you propose that staff from your company visit schools to give short workshops. The students benefit, you get to do something you care about, and you raise your organisation's profile. Or maybe you believe strongly in reducing your impact on the environment. You talk to your senior manager about getting together a committee of like-minded staff. Together you explore ways to change your company's purchasing procedures and practices. Donating that ugly mug to the staff room is an easy way to ditch disposables.

Option three: Your job is not aligned with your purpose, but you volunteer

Volunteering or joining a community group in an area you care about is a fantastic way to use your recreation time to actively recover from stress at work. Put the word out with the specifics of what sort of volunteering you'd like to do.

Option four: You plan a career change

This could be a sideways move in your own company, or to a similar role in another industry. A career counsellor or executive coach can be a tremendous help. In the meantime, simply taking relevant courses and making new connections in the area you want to move are both good for your wellbeing.

How I found my purpose

As I mentioned in the Introduction, my time in a specialist military unit means I understand high-performance environments.

While behind enemy lines in Somalia, I had to learn how to repeatedly switch on and switch off, alternating between the highest levels of performance and the recovery that let me sustain that performance. There were many things I loved about being in service, including supporting my peers to reach their own peak performance. However, I had also experienced a lot of trauma. Somalia left me in a spin. After being in active combat and witnessing the suffering in the local community – one I felt connected to, being of African heritage – I knew I needed to leave.

I spent the next ten years trying to find what my purpose in life was. What was the next stepping stone that would be in alignment with my purpose? I was re-engaging with who I was, and my mind was cloudy. It took me a long time for me to realise I was out of alignment.

Eventually, I found a calling in fitness and wellbeing. It was a great fit for my talents and my values. Now, I use my expertise in health and coaching to help others perform at their best and protect their wellbeing. I love arming people with the tools to sustain their health and keep performing at their best by making incremental changes, and watching them transform.

In return, working in alignment with my values means I'm thriving in my own personal and professional life.

What's the relationship between your purpose, your performance and your health?

Purpose increases your wellbeing, and wellbeing produces higher, more sustainable performance. No matter what your individual purpose is, you'll need to be healthy and well to fulfil it.

People who create greater alignment between their work and their purpose usually have higher wellbeing and life satisfaction. They cope better with the pressures of work and have a greater sense of achievement.

Your next steps

Achieving alignment between your purpose and your day-to-day activities takes time. What are some tiny steps you can take in the next one to two weeks?

Which one is *your* first step?

- Book a coffee date with yourself to ponder your course of action
- Mention to your family that you're thinking of making some changes
- Make an appointment with a health professional and/or executive coach

If there are new behaviours you'd like to adopt or habits to get rid of, I'll show you how to make that happen in the next chapter.

CHAPTER 2: THE MINDSET THAT MAKES HABIT CHANGE EASIER

Hopefully you're already inspired to make changes to live more in line with your values, strengths and skills. Adopting new ways of living and working can be daunting, especially if you've previously tried new routines without success. This chapter is here to help by showing you how to make changing your habits easier.

Be realistic

Make it ridiculously achievable

The first step is to take care when choosing the habit you want to take up or give up.

High performing professionals often have big goals, including goals for their wellbeing and work-life agility. When it comes to making lifelong lifestyle changes, fight against this overachieving instinct. To give yourself every chance of success, make your initial goal easy. Make it so easy you know you can definitely achieve it.

You think you can do more? Yes, you probably can, but start with something that seems ridiculously achievable.

Need more vegetables in your life? Don't set yourself up for failure by vowing to bring a salad every day if you're currently in a pie-and-chips routine. One of my clients, a manager in an accounting firm, started by simply packing a side salad to go with her takeaway lunch, even if it was just a handful of cherry tomatoes. By setting the bar low, she was more likely to start and keep moving in her desired direction after embedding the beginnings of a healthy new routine.

Here are some more examples of how to use achievable stepping stones to move towards your ultimate goal.

Unrealistic goal (for now)	Achievable stepping stone	First step
Eat 2.5 cups of vegetables a day	Pack a side salad on Mondays	Google 'easy workday salads'
Do yoga every day	Go to yoga class after work twice a month	Text a friend about doing classes together
Never bringing work home	Set work aside at 9pm each night	Download an app that limits access to your emails

Take stock of the rewards and costs

Being realistic also means being honest with yourself about the perks and the costs of your habits. Build these into your plan. For example, if you want to reduce your smoking, one of the rewards you might need to consider is the social side of a cigarette break. To replace this perk, you could ask a non-smoking colleague to help you by walking to the café for a takeaway coffee with you.

It's important to consider the downsides according to you, not just what other people say. Maybe the big downside from your perspective of smoking is that it's stopping you meet a new partner. Being honest with yourself about this will be more motivating than the doctor nagging you to quit.

Coming back to our three new 'achievable stepping stones' above, here are some of the costs and rewards for each.

New habit	Costs	Rewards
Pack a side salad on Mondays	time and effort in grocery shopping taking time on Sunday night to chop some veggies	experience more energy reduced risk of disease looking healthier over time
Go to yoga class after work twice a month	effort to pack yoga clothes and bring them to work less free time after work financial cost ($20) seeing less of your family that night	greater muscle endurance greater flexibility improved posture reduced aches and pains increased mental wellbeing
Set work aside at 9pm each night	anxiety about tasks you haven't completed annoyance from colleagues/bosses still expecting you to respond to emails late at night less time feeling professionally productive	more time for relaxation or active recovery more time with family more restful sleep increased mental wellbeing

Be kind to yourself

Remember that relapse is normal

The process of changing behaviour, as described in the Transtheoretical Model of Change, shows us that messing up is normal. It is entirely predictable that some Mondays you'll forget your salad. Or you just can't be bothered. Some days, you'll be working until midnight, and also realise you haven't been to yoga in weeks.

Knowing that this is part of the typical process of changing habits makes it easier to deal with. Anticipating relapse lets you prepare to handle yourself with compassion.

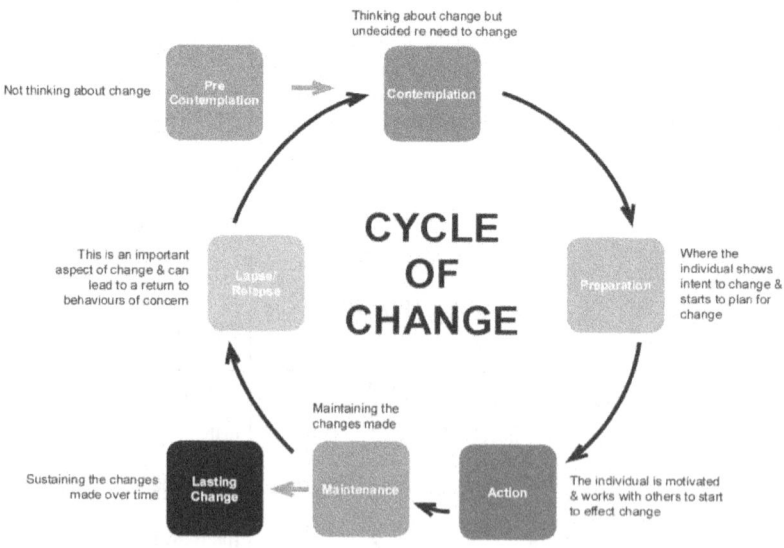

Show yourself some compassion

When you do mess up and revert to your old habits, remember that beating yourself up rarely leads to long-term success. Research has shown that people who have greater self-compassion have healthier habits. Being self-compassionate in a difficult moment means:

- **kindness** – treating yourself kindly
- **common humanity** – remembering that people all around the world have gone through what you're experiencing
- **mindfulness** – observing our negative feelings and thoughts without trying to suppress them

Self-compassion is *not* feeling sorry for yourself or letting yourself 'get away with' things. It means being understanding of yourself while continuing to do what's in your best interests, or in line with the values you identified in Chapter 2.

Let's say a good mate of yours has set a goal to complete a half marathon. You catch up for coffee and your friend is down because they've fallen off the rails. They're really annoyed with themselves because last month they were stressed with work and also had time off sick. They missed weeks of training and comforted themselves with chips and wine on the couch. What would you say? Would it be less judgmental than the things you would usually say to yourself in a similar situation? This is the type of compassion you can apply to yourself.

How Stacy finally started meditating

Stacy, aged 35, knew meditating was good for her. She had seen the research showing regular meditation reduces stress and physically changes your brain. She could certainly do with some help in the stress department. She felt a lot of pressure in her role managing an ever-expanding Work Health & Safety team with several difficult personalities, while at home, her seven-year-old stepson kept her on her toes too. Making meditation part of her routine and sticking to it seemed as impossible as it was necessary.

Stacy's previous New Year's resolution was to meditate for 20 minutes every evening. However, by the time she finished tidying up the kitchen after dinner and sending a few work emails, all she wanted to do was sleep. This time, she set a more realistic goal to meditate for five minutes every morning. And she set a smaller stepping-stone goal to start with just two minutes of meditation every work day.

Stacy knew that the demands of her family's morning routine would get in the way of her meditating at home, so decided to start by meditating in her car when she arrived at work. Her very first step was to google 'two-minute meditation' and she found that there were plenty of options that would guide her through the two minutes and make sure she still got into work on time.

Stacy was amazed at how that two-minute pause allowed her to walk into work with more calm and focus. As a reward, she treated herself to a proper lunch break in the park on Friday after her first week of meditating.

Of course, it wasn't all smooth sailing. On Monday morning during the second week, Stacy completely forgot. She was annoyed with herself for breaking her 'perfect' run but promised herself she would do it later. Unsurprisingly, that didn't happen. But then she remembered the benefits of self-compassion, and that everyone messes up when introducing a new habit. She relaxed and set a phone reminder to complete her two-minute meditation the next morning.

Check those limiting beliefs

Whenever we try to do something new or change a long-held way of behaving, we often have doubts about whether we can do it.

Unfortunately, it can be difficult to change these habitual thoughts that keep us stuck. It doesn't help that our brains like to focus on information that confirms our pre-existing beliefs.

Your brain is not telling you the whole truth

Our brains are constantly taking in an overwhelming amount of data and can't possibly process it all. One of the ways our brains decide what to pay attention to is by homing in on information that confirms our beliefs. Psychologists refer to this mental shortcut as 'confirmation bias'. A handy way to think of it is that our beliefs are the radio tuner, which helps us tune into different broadcasts of reality. All the stations are on the air at the same time, but we only pick up the ones we're tuned into.

For example, perhaps you saw a slim woman at a café eating a brownie and thought, 'How unfair, some people can eat anything they want without gaining weight.' You may not have noticed that she only ate a few forkfuls and shared the rest with her companion.

Or maybe you feel like a fraud in your job, especially because your boss rarely tells you she's happy with your work and has plenty of 'suggestions' for improvement. Meanwhile, you haven't noticed that your boss is hard on everyone and subscribes to the school of thought that you don't need to be told you're doing well.

The simple process in this section can help you recognise your fearful thoughts and limiting beliefs are not necessarily true. It allows you to explore these thoughts in such a way that they simply loosen their grip on you.

1. Identify a worry, concern, or belief that is getting in your way

It can be something related to work, relationships, your health, etc.

2. Is it really true?

Whenever you notice an unhelpful belief that's stopping you make progress, you need to ask yourself is whether it's really true. There are some common ways our thoughts get warped and twisted, called cognitive distortions. Check whether any of these apply.

Overgeneralising

This is when you take one instance and apply it to all situations, saying, 'I never get on top of my to-do list' or 'I always end up drinking more than I said I would.' Instead, focus on the situation at hand what actions you need to take right now.

Black-and-white thinking
Believing something or someone can only be good or bad, right or wrong, with no shades of grey in between. *'I had hot chips and now my whole eating plan is ruined.'* Instead, recognise that everything falls on a continuum.

Labelling
Giving yourself or someone else a negative label, which then shapes how you see yourself or them. *'I'm a stress-head by nature.'* Instead, look for evidence that this isn't always true.

Using 'Should' or 'Must'
When you tell yourself you *should* or *must* do something, you are usually setting too high a standard and end up feeling guilty. *'I should be able to run further.'* Instead, consciously choose to either do something or to *not* do it. If thinking about someone else's behaviour, replace 'should' with 'it would be nice if'. *'It would be nice if my boss told me when I had done a good job.'*

Mind reading
You make assumptions about what someone else thinks, even though you can't read their mind. *'My partner is sick of me spending my evenings at the gym.'* Instead of assuming, take the time to ask others what they think and tell them what you think.

What is the payoff?
The belief might be limiting you, but at the same time, there's

probably a benefit you get from holding it. Maybe believing that hot chips ruined your eating plan gives you an excuse to wash them down with a milkshake.

What is it costing you?
How do you react when you think that thought or belief? How does it alter your attitude, or who you are? What do you think, how do you feel, what images come to mind when you believe it? How do you treat others when you think it? How do you treat yourself when you think it? Does this thought take you further away or closer to your personal values and purpose?

Who would you be without that thought?
Try to imagine as vividly as possible what life would be like if you could literally not think this thought or belief anymore. How would your life be different?

Turn the thought around
Reverse the thought to create a positive message. If your thought was: *'I'm always too busy to take regular breaks,'* then the thought becomes, *'I'm never too busy to take regular breaks.'* And then ask yourself if that new thought is as true as or truer than the original one.

Look for evidence of this new thought
Where are some examples that this new thought is already true in your life?

After examining your limiting beliefs, you will usually find you have more flexibility in how you respond to problematic areas of life, and can achieve better outcomes in future.

Look for what's going well

As you work on transforming your lifestyle to better support sustainable high performance, training yourself to acknowledge what's going well provides ongoing motivation and reinforcement.

You will have heard about the benefits of calling to mind things for which we're grateful. People who practice gratitude are happier and healthier, build strong relationships and cope better with setbacks.

Some people like to keep a gratitude journal in a notebook or in an app, or by taking photos of things they're grateful for. Others use a family or workplace 'gratitude jar' – each person writes one thing they're grateful for on a slip of paper and pops it in the jar. Reading through the collection at the end of the year, or each month, becomes a special event. Writing thank you notes – anything from a quick text to a multi-page letter – is another way to reap the benefits of gratitude for both yourself and others.

If you're the journaling type, you could extend your questions to focus specifically on your work-life agility journey. For example, each day in a special notebook you could record and give yourself a pat on the back for:

- something you're grateful for
- something you did well at work
- something you did to improve your wellbeing

If you struggle with the strategies suggested in this chapter, or frequently feel 'out of sorts' emotionally, see a registered counsellor or your GP.

Two bonus tips for behaviour change

1. Have a contingency plan

Know what can go wrong. For instance, if you plan to go for a walk three days a week and bad weather may stop you from doing so, have a set of exercises you know you can complete at home. What else could impede on your plan? How might you plan around these factors?

2. Start somewhere on no-motivation days

You will run into days where you just can't be bothered. It happens. Rather than giving up entirely, start *somewhere*. If you planned to go for a run, put your running shoes on. If you planned to clean the house, start by wiping down the table. Small actions have a tendency to flow on into other actions. You may be more likely to step outside and go for a 10 minute walk. You may be more likely to wipe down the kitchen bench too.

Be patient, be persistent, and remember to look at the bigger picture. Something is better than nothing. See how you go.

CHAPTER 3: EATING WELL FOR WORK–LIFE AGILITY

If you feel like you could improve your eating habits, you're in good company. The Australian Bureau of Statistics shows only one in 20 Australians eat enough fruit and vegetables. Your health, vitality and performance depend on a nutritious diet.

Without the nutrients and sustainable energy from eating well, it won't be easy to recover from stress, perform at your best and enjoy quality of life.

What is a healthy diet anyway?

You might be confused about what healthy eating means, and which 'experts' to believe. Should we all be eating vegan now, or avoiding fat, or quitting sugar or eating kale with every meal? The Australian Dietary Guidelines are the best evidence-based information on what a healthy diet looks like.

The Australian Guide to Healthy Eating (part of the Australian

Dietary Guidelines) doesn't use the old food pyramid, but a plate. The plate shows that, for good health, the bulk of our meals need to be made up of vegetables, legumes and wholegrains. The rest of the plate is made up of meat, fish, eggs, nuts, dairy foods and fruit. We can also eat the 'sometimes' foods in small amounts. 'Sometimes' foods include drinks other than water – juice, soft drink, wine – and 'junk foods' like chips, lollies, biscuits, cakes and chocolate.

From time to time, different fads argue that we should ditch dairy, wheat or sugar (even to the point of avoiding fruit). However, one thing that everyone agrees on is that eating plant-based foods is vital. And considering the stats above on how few of us are eating enough fruit and vegetables, almost everyone can benefit from eating more plants.

Why you should 'eat a rainbow'

According to the Australian Dietary Guidelines, we need, 'plenty of vegetables of different types and colours'. Our bodies need access to the whole *rainbow* of plants, every day. Eating carrot sticks by the kilo won't bring the same benefits of eating a variety of coloured plants – including the roots, leaves and legumes.

Different colours provide different vital nutrients. For example, we need red plants for the antioxidant lycopene, yellow for beta-carotene, green for vitamins C and K, purple for the anthocyanin flavonoids, and brown or white vegetables too, like onions, for vitamin B7, and cauliflower for vitamin C.

We need to eat vegetables every day because we need a supply of their different types of fibre, vitamins and phytonutrients (plant chemicals) every day, throughout the day.

Avoiding the blood sugar rollercoaster

Another benefit of eating plenty of vegetables and wholegrains is the impact of fibre on blood sugar. Fibre helps you avoid the peaks and troughs in your blood sugar levels.

Your body works hard to keep your blood sugar stable. When you start to use up the sugar in your blood, your body uses a hormone (glucagon) to break down stored energy and bring your blood sugar levels back up. When you eat, your blood sugar also rises, so your body uses insulin to store the excess sugar (as glycogen or fat).

If you eat foods that break down too quickly, like processed carbohydrate foods, your body can overdo the insulin. Too much energy is stored and you feel tired when your blood sugar crashes. You may then be drawn to sugary foods to give yourself a lift, creating an unhelpful blood-sugar rollercoaster.

Wholegrains, legumes and seeds are your ticket to a steady, long-lasting supply of energy. Think brown rice, rolled oats, barley, quinoa, peanut butter, lentils and chickpeas. Wholegrains are as important to our health as vegetables. According to a review of 49 studies, they reduce your chances of heart disease, diabetes, abdominal fat, and some cancers.

Adding plenty of vegetables and some fat to a meal also helps maintain stable blood sugar. Including healthy fats is as easy as adding some nuts on top of your porridge, or some avocado to your crackers.

Eating for gut health

In recent years, research has exploded into the relationship between our health and our microbiome. Our microbiome is the community of bacteria and other microrganisms living inside us. While we still have much to uncover, one thing that's clear is that having a diverse microbiome is related to better health.

So, what foods support a flourishing community of helpful bacteria in your gut? While fermented foods like sauerkraut and kombucha have become popular (and may be helpful), the main answer, once again, is plants. Your helpful gut bacteria thrive on the fibre in vegetables, legumes, nuts and seeds. Conversely, eating too many 'sometimes' foods can damage your gut health. These foods are typically low in fibre, high in simple sugars and saturated fats, and don't allow your microbiome to flourish.

What about vegetarian and vegan diets?

According to Google search data, interest in veganism is at an all-time high. We're currently searching for information on eating vegan about 3 times more often than we did 5 years ago.

Personally, I've recently been experimenting with eating a more vegetarian diet. Being a born-and-bred carnivore, giving up the steak and eating more plant foods hasn't been easy, but I've felt so much better for it. I'm experiencing less brain fog, and no longer go into a 'food coma' after a big BBQ lunch.

If you do follow a strict vegan diet (with no animal products at all), it can be hard to get enough iron, vitamin B12 and calcium, but a dietitian can help.

What to drink

If plant foods like fruits and vegetables are full of healthy nutrients, doesn't that mean you should drink juices as often as possible? Actually, it doesn't. Water is the best drink. Start with a glass at breakfast, follow it up with one at every meal, and use water as a reason to hop out of your chair during the day.

Of course, it's fine to have a juice from time to time but remember it lacks most of the vital fibre that whole fruits and vegetables have. Juice also has a lot more energy than a piece of fruit, which might be stored as body fat. You probably only eat one apple at a time, but one glass of juice might include three or four apples. So, most of the time, it's best to *eat* your fruit and drink your water.

Tea is another nutritious drink, with helpful antioxidants. You can enjoy a whole variety of black, green, white and herbal teas. Are you more of a java fan? Coffee also contains antioxidants. Just be mindful of how much milk you're drinking as most of us don't need the extra calories. Sticking to the smallest size cup at the café is a healthy habit to have.

Practical strategies to make healthy eating automatic

Healthy eating starts with setting yourself up for success by changing the physical environment around you. First, stock your kitchen with healthy staples. Ensure your house contains all the foods you need, and none that you don't.

Some healthy groceries to have on stand-by for quick and nutritious meals include:
- tinned chickpeas, lentils or other beans
- baked beans
- tinned tomatoes and pasta sauce
- tinned tuna or chicken
- dried fruit (dates, figs, sultanas, apricots, etc.)
- nuts and seeds (walnuts, almonds, macadamia nuts, sunflower seeds, pumpkin seeds etc.)
- peanut butter
- olive oil and vinegar
- brown rice
- quinoa
- eggs
- stir-fry meat
- frozen vegetables
- frozen berries
- frozen salmon

Next, make your workday foolproof. Search for ideas and get together a list of your favourite healthy meals and snacks for work and keep the ingredients on hand. Bliss balls, for example, are easy to make and to transport to work. Homemade meals and snacks are almost always more nutritious than takeaway or restaurant meals.

Travelling for work? Having nutrient-dense snacks can save you from buying unhealthy options from the airport or mini bar. Dried fruit and nuts, muesli bars, beef jerky, peanut butter on rice cakes and apples are easy to carry in your bag. On the plane, consider ordering the vegetarian option.

Whether at home or away, sometimes you want to order a takeaway dinner, and you can choose the more nutritious options. For example:
- Indian: Lentil dahl
- Pizza: Vegetarian
- Thai: Tom Yum Soup with prawns or chicken
- Pub: Small steak with vegetables
- Fish and chips: Grilled fish with salad, small chips to share

If you're dining out, think ahead. If you have a say over where you're eating, aim for a venue with healthy options. Then download the menu and decide what to order before being put on the spot. Adding a side salad is always a good idea. Feel free to order dessert but consider sharing it with a friend – and be sure to take time to savour it.

How healthy eaters think

If you want to make nutritious eating a habit, it helps to get your head in the right space.

First, if you want to improve your eating habits, be wary of adopting a dieting approach. When you focus on restricting what types of food you eat and how much, it almost inevitably leads to rebound overeating. Due to physical hunger and psychological deprivation, you end up eating more than you would have if you hadn't deprived yourself. We have known for a long time that if something is a 'forbidden fruit' it makes it only more tempting, so you end up worse off than you were before.

A healthy eating mindset makes room for small treats. No food is ever totally 'off limits'. When you deliberately and mindfully enjoy small portions of your favourite 'sometimes' foods, you break free of the guilt and deprivation cycle. Many dieters have been 'on' and then 'off' a diet dozens of times over their lifetime. Research in the prestigious journal *Nature* shows most dieters gain back half of the lost weight in the first year after losing it. Much of the rest gain it back within the next three years.

Rather than dieting, healthy eating is something you do continuously, and it works for life. Healthy eaters make small improvements they can stick with for the long term, rather than big changes they put up with for only a short time.

Healthy people also think for themselves when deciding what to eat. They stick to the basic principles of healthy eating rather than fads. For example, don't get distracted by trying to eat lots of superfoods. 'Superfood' is a marketing term. So-called superfoods like spirulina, krill oil, chia seeds and coconut water are nutritious but not essential. Plain old carrots and baked beans are nutritious too. Similarly, foods sold as 'low fat' seem healthier but the fat is often replaced with extra sugar or salt to boost the flavour. Some foods are 'sugar-free' due to artificial sweeteners. Research shows we eat larger serves of 'diet' foods anyway. These marketing tactics distract you from the bigger picture of a balanced diet.

If you're ever confused by what to eat for good health and to maintain a healthy weight, keep it simple. Go for uncomplicated, unprocessed food in its most natural state.

Ask yourself:
- In the ingredients list, can I see real foods listed?
- Can I see many ingredients that sound more like chemicals?
- Is this food close to its natural form, or has it been heavily processed?
- Would my great-grandmother recognise this as food?
- Could I easily make a simple version of this at home instead (with less salt, sugar, additives)?

How much food is enough?

Do you need to reduce your weight to be in the healthy range? There are some practical ways to eat smaller portions without feeling you're restricting yourself. For example:
- Choose good quality, nutritious food and savour it – this will make it more satisfying
- Start with a small serve – you can always eat more if you need it

- Use your smallest plates and bowls – small serves will look large enough
- Check in with your belly before and during the meal: how hungry are you?
- Enjoy a delicious dessert by sharing it

How Ruth maintained a healthier weight

Ruth was 32 years old and very busy in her role as a senior HR Manager. Despite her full schedule, she still managed to exercise two to three times a week. She also had a large group of 'social butterflies' among her friends who loved to eat out, and to set her up on dates. As a result, she ate out three to four times a week at different restaurants and drank large amounts of alcohol. She was overweight and recognised her weight was impacting her health. Exercise alone wasn't enough to manage her weight. She had attempted to diet many times in the past, but soon regained the weight after ending each diet.

I helped Ruth keep an eating diary for one week to assess her eating habits, times, quality and frequency of meals, alcohol and water intake. Based on Ruth's weight-loss goals, we developed a nutritious eating plan that fit within her busy work schedule and social life. We made sure it was realistic, enjoyable and sustainable for her over the long term. For example, she learned how to make smart choices when ordering at restaurants, and to savour that one glass of wine.

Ruth is still following the principles and education of the

eating plan we created for her over two years ago. She's lost three dress sizes and maintained that healthier weight. She has an abundance of energy to bring to work and social engagements.

An honest audit of your eating habits

To know what changes will give you the best return on your effort, first you need to take stock of your habits.

1. Keep a food diary

Do this for at least one full day, ideally for three days. Keep a list in the notes section of your phone (or on paper if you prefer) of everything you eat. Everything. If you have sugar in your coffee, make a note. If you finished your kid's breakfast, write it down. List the mayonnaise you added to your sandwich and the mints you grabbed from the jar at work.

Most importantly, do it without judgment or self-criticism. Being mindful of what you eat means being aware without being judgmental. You're simply taking stock.

2. Learn from your diary

When you recorded what you ate, did anything surprise you? Are you eating a lot more or less of certain foods? Are you eating 2.5 cups of vegetables every day?

Would you say your meals resemble the healthy eating plate? (Mostly wholegrains and vegetables, with some fruit, meats, eggs, seafood, legumes, dairy, nuts and seeds?)

3. Doable changes

What are the most achievable changes you could make that would have the most impact?

For example, if you have a large coffee every morning, could you be happy with a regular coffee? If you're not having any vegetables at lunch, could you start buying a small side salad with your sandwich? Swap from less nutritious white rice and white bread to brown rice and wholemeal bread? What about packing a few nuts and dried figs for an afternoon snack?

Remember, while it's tempting to overhaul your routine, overwhelming changes are unlikely to stick.

For support specific to your situation and your dietary needs, there is plenty of qualified help out there. Book in with a dietitian, GP, lifestyle coach or psychologist.

CHAPTER 4: PHYSICAL MOVEMENT FOR MENTAL PERFORMANCE

It's probably no surprise that moving your body is vital to your health, but have you thought about how physical fitness is necessary for work–life agility? Your chances of achieving sustainable high performance and quality of life are dramatically boosted with a regular exercise routine.

The mind–body connection

Sometimes we forget that our brains are part of our body, but when your body is thriving, your brain will function better too. Your brain, like every organ in your body, needs a good supply of oxygen and nutrients to do its best work. Then it needs adequate recovery to do it again the next day.

Our physical activity influences our cognitive abilities – like problem-solving, analysing and creative thinking – as well as our emotional health. The mind–body connection works the other way too. Our thoughts, beliefs and feelings can influence how our body functions and feels. For example, mental tension often manifests as muscular tension or digestive issues. People who experience chronic pain can find some relief using psychological strategies. It's another reason to invest time in mental recovery activities to boost your physical health (see more in the next chapter).

Movement for sustainable high performance

Do you sometimes struggle with fatigue and wish you had more energy to accomplish more each day? Getting moving could have a significant difference. A University of Georgia study found that inactive people could decrease their fatigue by 65% and boost their energy levels by 20% through low-intensity exercise. A mere 20 minutes of leisurely walking three times a week was enough to achieve this effect.

Moving your body also helps your brain think more clearly. It's thought walking boosts your decision-making power when you're under the pump by increasing the oxygen in the parts of the brain that need it. In a New Zealand study, researchers gave healthy young women a tough mental task. They also asked about their usual exercise habits. The women who exercised more made significantly faster and more accurate decisions.

Other research from Stanford University shows exercise helps your creativity flow. Participants were given tough creative thinking tasks. Some were assigned to walk around while completing the tasks, and these participants produced more creative ideas while walking, and also shortly after. The study also found that walking outdoors provided the most original and highest quality ideas.

Of course, walking is not the only physical activity that helps you improve your performance. Any form of exercise will help your brain receive more oxygen.

Movement as stress management

One of the major benefits of exercise for busy professionals is its direct effect on stress levels. Working out helps to reduce your levels of stress hormones, like adrenalin and cortisol. It also releases endorphins, your body's natural pain killers that produce that 'high' after a tough workout.

Getting your blood flowing and including stretching in your workout also combats muscle tension. A hectic day probably leaves you with tightness, especially in your neck and shoulders. This can lead to pain, but movement can help you let the tension go. If you still have pain, check in with your physiotherapist.

Other health benefits

No doubt you've heard of the other benefits of regular exercise, but it never hurts to remind ourselves. Doctors are increasingly prescribing exercise like they prescribe medications to help their patients:
- maintain a healthy weight
- reduce their risk of heart disease, diabetes, cancer

- improve their mental health
- sleep better
- improve their strength, flexibility and balance for daily activities
- increase their energy
- keep their bones and muscles strong

Activities that strengthen your muscles are especially vital if you're aiming to lose weight. Without muscle-strengthening movement, you will lose a higher proportion of invaluable muscle alongside excess fat. Once you've lost this fuel-burning muscle mass, it's harder to maintain a healthy weight in future.

How much is enough?

Physical activity guidelines say that to stay healthy, adults need to:
- take part in 2.5 to 5 hours of moderate intensity activity, or 1.25 to 2.5 hours of vigorous intensity activity (or an equivalent combination), **every week**
- be active on most days, preferably **every day**
- do muscle strengthening activities on at least **two days a week**

If your current exercise program is mainly made up of running for the bus, don't worry. Any physical activity is better than doing none. Physical activity doesn't have to be formal exercise either. Anything that gets your body moving and makes your heart beat faster is helpful. Every few minutes you add to your day will help, and you can build up gradually.

What's 'moderate' and what's 'vigorous' activity?

Moderate intensity activity takes a bit of effort, but you can still talk. It could be going for a brisk walk or taking an active yoga class, or chores at home (think scrubbing the bath or raking leaves).

Vigorous intensity means you're huffing and puffing. You might be running, cycling, playing ball sports, boxing or working with a personal trainer. Because the intensity is higher, you don't need to spend as long on these more energetic activities.

Don't forget the recommended two days a week of muscle strengthening activities. You can do weights in a gym or body-weight exercises at home; work with a personal trainer or join a CrossFit group; or get stuck into digging in the garden or helping a friend move house. When I was in the military, we would sometimes do hundreds of push-ups in a day and run 10 km carrying weighted backpacks. But for the average person, the physical activity guidelines say there's no reason to do long, strenuous workouts every day.

You can easily meet the guidelines with a weekly routine that fits into your jam-packed schedule.

Here are some examples that combine moderate and vigorous intensity exercise with muscle strengthening:

- **The lunch break routine**: 20 minutes walking x three days a week, plus two x 30-minute personal training sessions
- **The variety pack**: 15 minutes home yoga, 30 minutes recreational swimming, 20 minutes weights at the gym, 30-minute high-intensity gym class, 20-minute walk to the café
- **The business traveller**: 20-minute walk at the airport, 30-minute hotel room workout, 30 minutes lifting weights in the hotel gym, 2 x 20-minute walk near the hotel

Before you get started on a new exercise regime, it's always recommended to get specific recommendations for your situation from a GP and an experienced trainer. This is especially important if you have particular health conditions or injuries.

The two-minute office workout

If you have a private office or an empty meeting room, here's a quick full-body workout that will help you get closer to your weekly exercise target. One of my busiest clients does a routine like this in his hotel room whenever he travels for work. Repeat it two or three times a day and you'll soon feel and see the difference. No change of clothes or equipment needed, but an exercise band is useful and easy to carry in your bag. Buy one from a sports store or physiotherapist.

Crank out as many repetitions in the time given as you can, and see if you can improve your numbers each time.

- 30 seconds of squats
- 30 seconds plank with shoulder taps
- 30 seconds of alternating lunges
- 30 seconds of push-ups (on knees or toes)

Follow with a quick stretch of the legs, buttocks, and chest. Have a look at the images below or ask a trainer to demonstrate correct technique.

Of course, you can put together your own two-minute workout using any of these exercises below. Just make sure you choose a balance of movements to work the whole body.

Simple indoor exercises

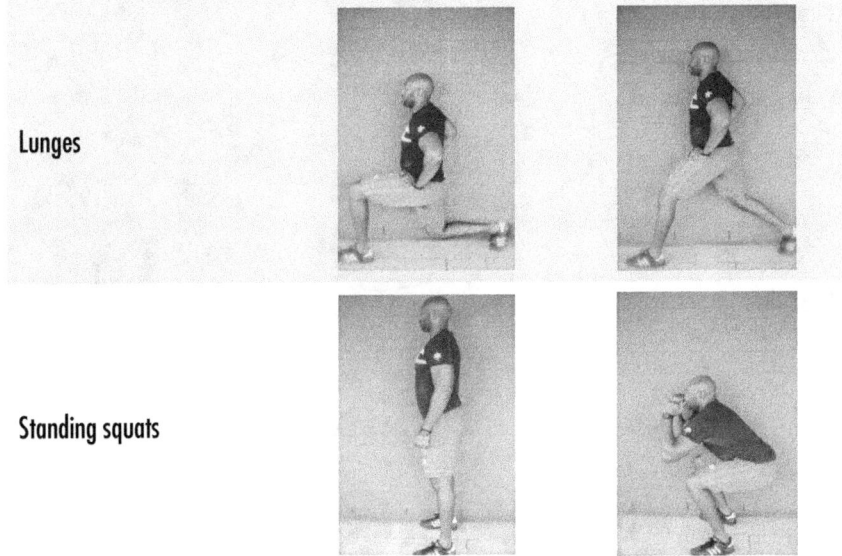

Lunges

Standing squats

Sit-to-stand

Wall squats

Bicep curls

Chair dips

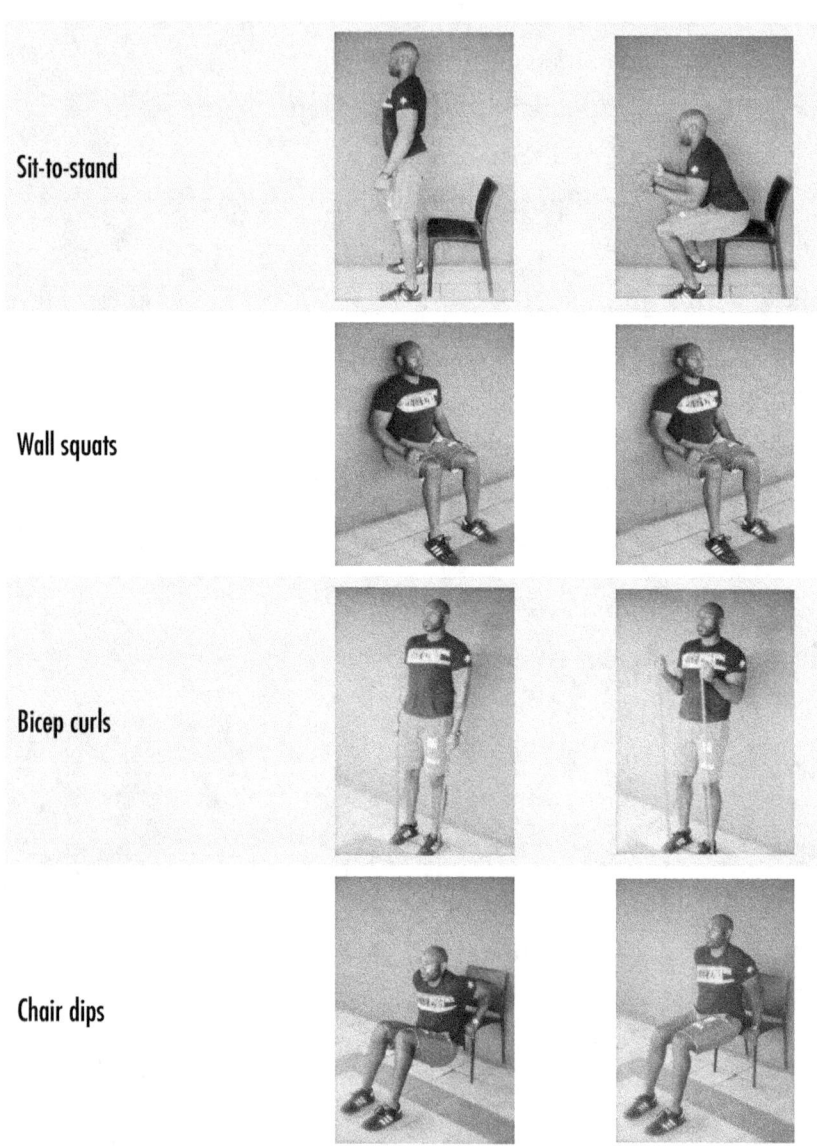

Shoulder press

Lateral shoulder raises

Wall push ups

Star jumps

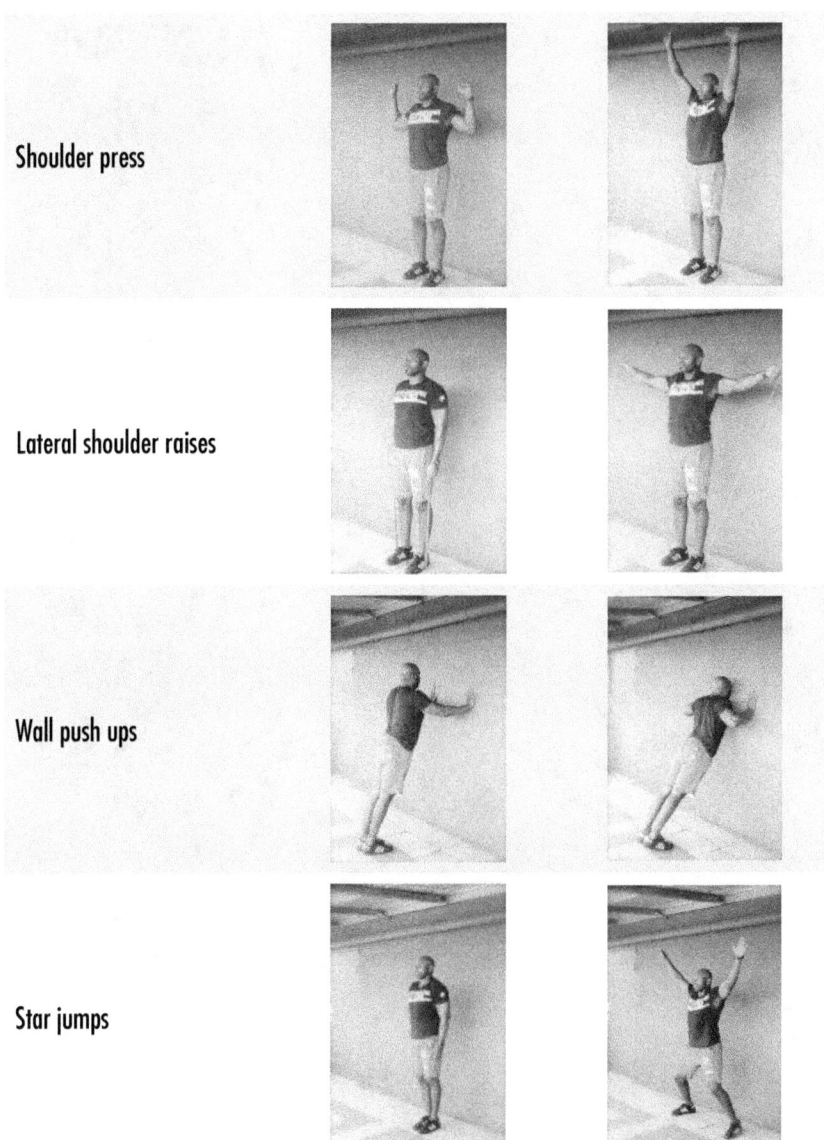

Ski shuffles

Burpees

Jogging on the spot

Step ups

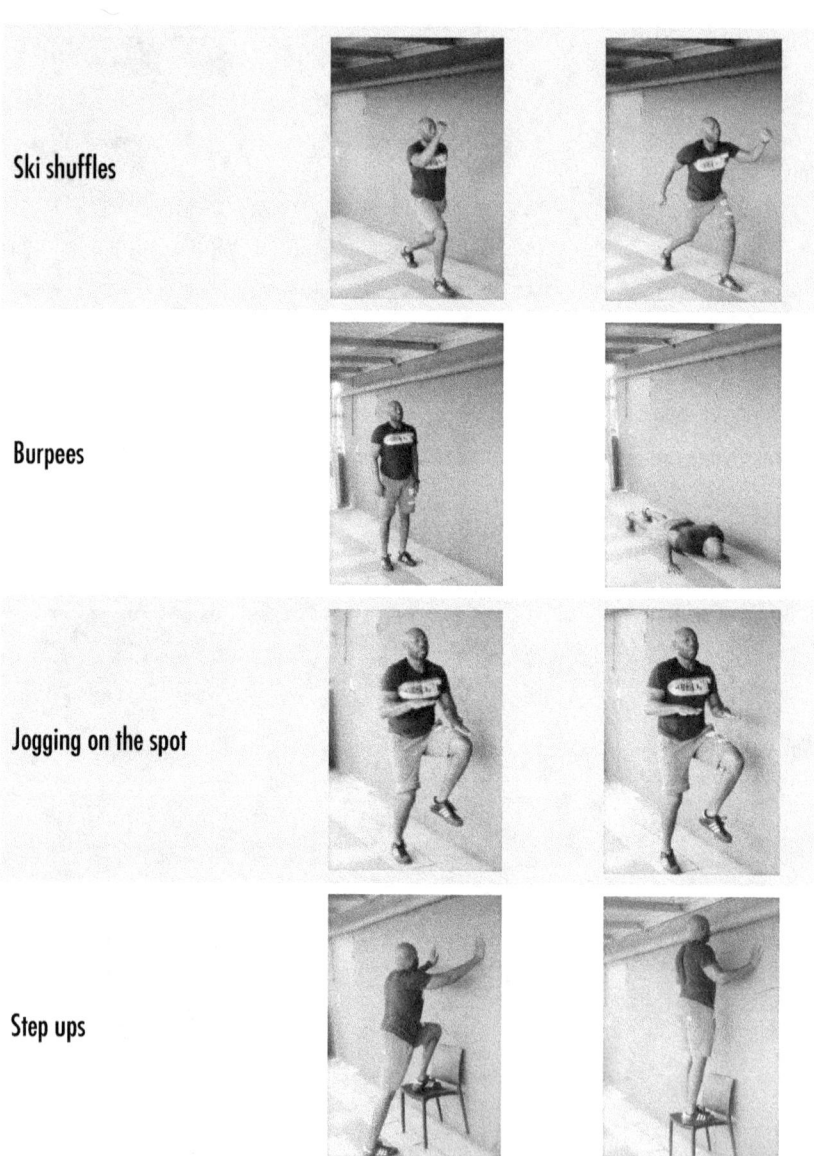

Glute bridge		
Single leg glute bridge		
Seated rows		
Crunches		
Leg raises		
Plank		
Push up		

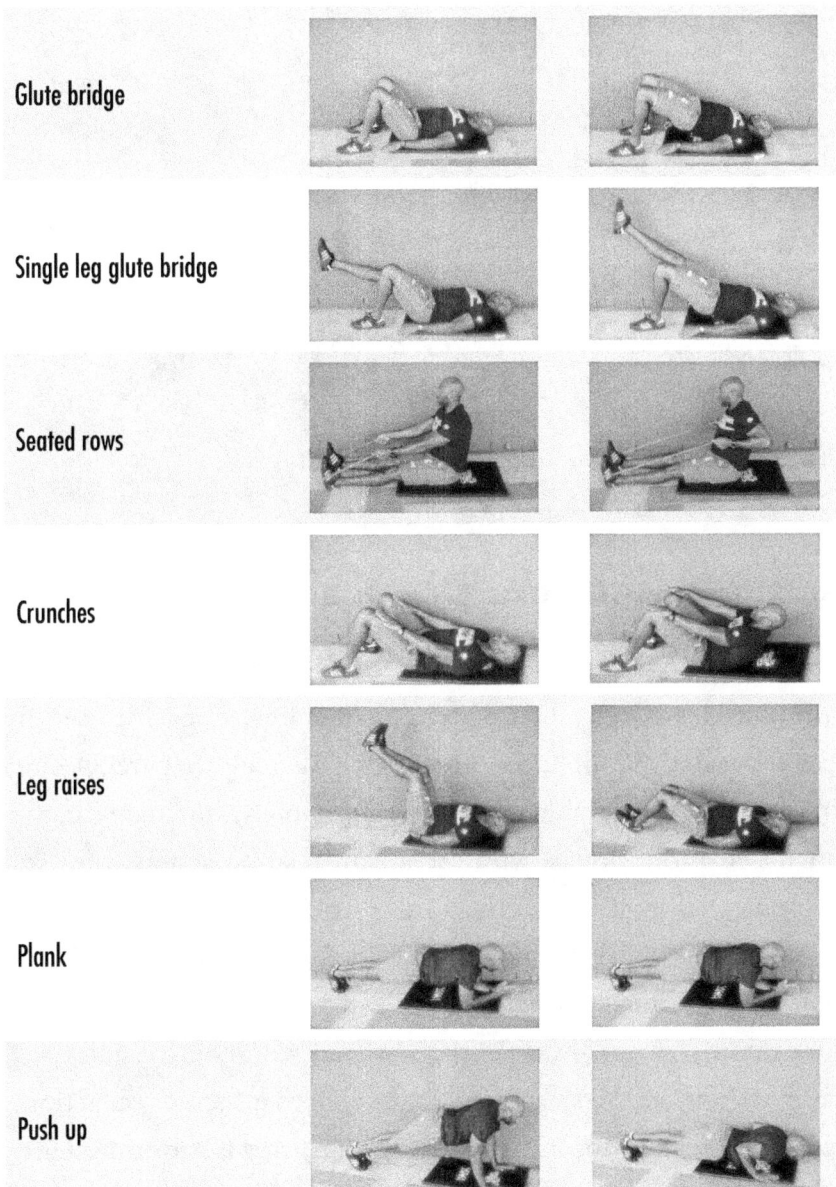

Push up

Equipment needed

Setting SMART exercise goals

If you tried in the past to vaguely 'exercise more' or 'get back into running', it's time to take a more deliberate approach to setting exercise goals. We all know it helps to have goals that are Specific, Measurable, Achievable, Relevant and Timely, but many highly organised professionals who use a similar approach at work still neglect to apply it to their health.

First, let's make sure your goal is focussed on your actions, not outcomes. Achieving a certain weight or a certain blood pressure, for example, is not always entirely within your control. However, your actions *are*. So start by setting a goal that focuses on actions, especially if you don't currently have an exercise routine. Later, you can focus on outcomes like doing 30 push-ups in a row, running 5 km or achieving a healthy Body Mass Index.

Specific

Of course, your goal also needs to be specific. So instead of 'exercise more', your goal might be, *'Exercise five days a week, including two days of muscle-strengthening exercise.'*

To be even more specific, think about what type of exercise you're happy to commit to. *'Exercise five days a week, including two days of weights at the gym and three days of either walking or cycling.'*

Measurable

To make it more measurable, add a time limit there. *'Exercise five days a week for at least 20 minutes.'*

Achievable

Next, check if that's achievable for you. Ask yourself, 'On a scale of one to ten, how confident am I that I can achieve that?' If you answered anything less than eight, work out what would help you succeed and feel more confident. Or change your goal.

Feeling overwhelmed with competing pressures in life? It's OK to downgrade your initial goal. For example, instead of five days a week, aim for three for now.

Relevant

Goals that feel relevant to you are more motivating than those imposed by someone else. Let's say your doctor says you have to exercise to take care of your heart. But that doesn't fire you up. Find your 'why' behind your desire to get moving. Is it because you need the stress-busting benefits so you can be a nicer person to your family? Is it because you think more clearly and have better ideas at work when you exercise? Or perhaps you want to make sure you're around to meet your grandkids one day.

Timely

When will you start? Do you need time to prepare yourself – to find a workout partner, or a trainer, to buy new shoes, or research the best places to walk near your office? Would you like to start with a 'practise' week and then commit to achieving your goal every week for the next month?

Your final goal might look like this:

> *'Starting next week, I will exercise three days a week for at least 20 minutes, including one day of weights at the gym and two days of either walking or cycling. I will do this every week for four weeks, then review my goal.'*

How to make exercise an easier habit

Setting exercise goals that are SMART will get you well on your way to successfully integrating exercise into your daily routine. Here are a few more strategies to make it even easier.

Stack your habits

Add helpful habits before or after something you already do. For example:

- When you're catching the train home, get off two stations earlier for a longer walk

- When you're getting ready for bed, lay out your workout clothes for the morning
- When you're planning the week ahead, plan when you'll exercise
- When you're arranging to see a friend, ask them to join you for a boxing session instead of a wine (or before the wine)
- When you're travelling for work, always go for a walk straight after checking in to your hotel
- When taking your usual coffee break during the workday, also do a two-minute office workout

Draw on social support

Involving other people is also a great motivation booster. If you've arranged to meet a friend for boxing or a walk, you'll have to think twice before cancelling. It also makes exercise more fun and an even better stress buster when you bring a friend along.

Talking about your goals with others is another powerful way to increase the chances of achieving them. Making your commitment public motivates you to follow through, plus it lets others know how they can help you.

How Phil used movement to regain his energy

Phil Jones, 46, is an accountant in a large firm. When I started working with Phil, he was overweight, on high blood pressure medication and low on energy. He struggled to even play and kick the ball around with his 12-year-old son for more than ten minutes.

To improve Phil's health and ability to perform at work, I implemented a movement program with incremental movement goals. At work, I started getting Phil to get up and move every hour, to the printer or the water bubbler. At home, he started to regularly stand up and drink water from the fridge.

I also coached him to start walking and then running in the morning and evening. We gradually increased his physical movement time from half an hour to one hour, three to four times a week. A short routine of bodyweight exercises complemented his running and developed his strength.

After several months of this increased exercise, we saw real changes in Phil's physical health. His doctor was able to reduce his high blood pressure medication. Slowly and steadily, he lost 15 kg in six months, and he had more energy and could focus at work for longer periods. Most important of all, he can now play and kick the ball around with his son.

Set your own SMART exercise goal

Write down your general exercise goals.

Choose one, be **Specific**
Is it **Measurable**?
Is it **Achievable**? How could you make it more achievable?
What makes it **Relevant**? What's your 'why'?
Make it **Timely.** When will you start?

CHAPTER 5: RECOVERY AND RESILIENCE

You probably got to where you are with grit and determination. You typically put in long hours and often push through fatigue. While an appetite for hard work might have helped you succeed, without a plan to stop and recharge it can be your downfall.

What is stress?

Stress is how our body responds when we are faced with challenging and sometimes dangerous situations. Before modern society, stress occurred when humans were faced with survival challenges, such as encountering predators. You may have heard of this – it is sometimes called the fight-or-flight response. Human bodies responded to a threat or challenge by preparing it to either physically attack the threat or escape it. In order to do this, the body:

- Releases adrenaline
- Increases heart rate
- Supplies increased blood to the muscles
- Increases breathing rate
- Slows or stops digestion
- Depresses the immune system
- Moves blood away from the 'thinking' part of our brain to the 'reacting' part of our brain

The problem is, our bodies respond in exactly the same way to modern stressors, such as making deadlines and paying the bills. What's more, most modern stressors are ongoing or chronic, which means our bodies may constantly be in fight-or-flight mode for a period of weeks, months or years. To you, this may feel like:

- Being 'on edge', nervous
- Pounding heart
- Feeling jittery, restless
- Muscle aches or tension
- Chest pains, anxiety
- Nausea, heartburn, ulcers, weight gain
- Getting sick more often or recovery from illness is slower
- Difficulties with concentration, memory, sleep

How to maximise an opportunity during isolation to recalibrate?

We all want to matter. We all want to feel like we're effective and have an impact on all that we care about. This desire is why we read self-help books, how to raise teenagers, go through leadership programs, professional development and the like. The intent is to develop our skills and capability. It's what I call, our craft. We want to keep sharpening our ability to empower, influence and lead others, outcomes and our future. What is often forgotten is that we first need to master leading ourselves as a foundation to achieving in these other domains. 'Leading self' lays a foundation that increases the probability of enjoying sustainable performance. There are 3 critical layers to leading self:

1. Self-compassion. This is a mindset I have struggled with most of my life. Self-compassion entails being kind to yourself, particularly when experiencing adversity. Being compassionate towards yourself means you acknowledge that you are deserving of good things, that you're worthy and enough, as you are, and you don't overly judge and criticise yourself for inadequacies or shortcomings. If we don't possess self-compassion, our inner critic is often overactive. It's the loudest voice. This inner critic is one reason why we self-sabotage. We're always trying to live-up to expectations and succeed. We must develop our inner coach. If we employed an executive coach or mentor that spoke to us the way we talk to ourselves, we'd fire them.

2. Purpose. Do you have one? Can you articulate it into a concrete statement? Do you know why you get out of bed each day? Or know your ultimate reason for being? Purpose builds resilience, leads to health and longevity. It can be our North Star that helps us avoid misalignment. Knowing what we care about across all aspects of our life and spending the time to articulate that through a purpose statement, can prevent the reactivity that suffocates us. It can help us prioritise and live each day in a manner that honours us and what we care about.
3. Energy. Do you possess the mental, emotional, physical and spiritual energy to be your best self? Do you strategically recover every day and night? Do you wake up feeling refreshed? Do you exercise regularly and eat well? Do you practice gratitude or mindfulness? If you're fatigued, your energy is obviously depleted. Without energy, we cannot function effectively. Our 'craft' is impaired. Managing and nurturing our energy must be prioritised. Whilst we know this, we struggle to do it. A lack of self-compassion and not knowing our why (your purpose), are linked to why we don't. If we want to change behaviour, we need to discover a strong enough motivator to do so. If you want to make change, channel Simon Sinek's mantra, 'Start with Why'!

During unprecedented times like Covid 19 or any other period. There are many challenges. However, this is a time where we can really recalibrate to absorb not only what's going on now, but to protect our future. It is valuable time to lead self and become an even better version of our current selves. Self-compassion, purpose and energy will help us do this.

Fight-or-flight in modern society

The physiological response to stress has persisted throughout thousands of years. The fight-or-flight response is hardwired. It allows us to automatically address dangerous or threatening situations quickly and with optimal physical and cognitive functioning.

The stressors we experience day to day are markedly different from the stressors our ancestors used to experience. While our ancient counterparts were commonly encountering stressors such as predators, food shortages, searching for water, and rival tribes, those frequent occurrences have now been replaced by office deadlines, long working hours, traffic jams and struggling to meet performance indicators. Would you rate these as equivalent threats to your wellbeing?

Unfortunately, despite massive technological, societal and infrastructural change over the last 25,000 years, our bodies and their functions have remained essentially unchanged. This means that you involuntarily react in exactly the same way to seeing an intruder in your home or reacting to an imminent car accident as you do to a looming deadline or an impromptu meeting with your boss. Two of these are an imminent survival threat; the other two are not. Despite this, the fight-or-flight response is still activated in both cases. Our bodies cannot tell the difference between a real survival threat and a perceived threat.

Long-term consequences of stress

When you keep your foot on the pedal and don't schedule deliberate recovery, symptoms of burnout inevitably emerge.

Since 2019, the World Health Organisation (WHO) now recognises burnout as a medical condition. The WHO says burnout is a syndrome resulting from workplace stress that hasn't been successfully managed. The symptoms include feeling exhausted, feeling negative or cynical about work, and being less able to do your job well. The problem of burnout isn't 'just in your head' either. The respectable journal *PLOS ONE* reports that other common consequences of burnout are cardiovascular disease, musculoskeletal pain and clinical depression.

If you think you might be at risk for burnout, you're in good company. Stress affects about five million Australians, according to research carried out by Roy Morgan for Medibank. The main causes of stress include a lack of sleep (44%), juggling too many things (36%) and pressure at work (39%). It is vital to proactively manage stress and include recovery in your daily routine.

The love–hate relationship between stress and performance

As well as the long-term consequences of poorly managed stress, stress can get in the way of you performing at your best right now.

At one end of the continuum, when you have low levels of stress and stimulation, your performance will be low too. Imagine you're at one of those meetings that could have been an email and doesn't seem relevant to you anyway. You'd be quite relaxed, and you wouldn't have bothered to prepare for the meeting or say much. You wouldn't achieve a lot.

On the other end, where you face high levels of stress and cognitive arousal, you still won't perform well on difficult tasks. For instance, in a high-pressure meeting you might stumble over your words, lose your cool, or forget the important points you wanted to make. Bear in mind that this effect applies to your team members too. Some employees who seem 'lazy' and unmotivated might in fact feel overwhelmed by their work, or other aspects of their life.

The sweet spot? Where you have enough stress to stimulate you but not so much it overwhelms you. What if you were going to an interview for a job you really wanted, and you had prepared thoroughly and consciously calmed your nerves beforehand? You'd be in a great place to perform at your best and win the job.

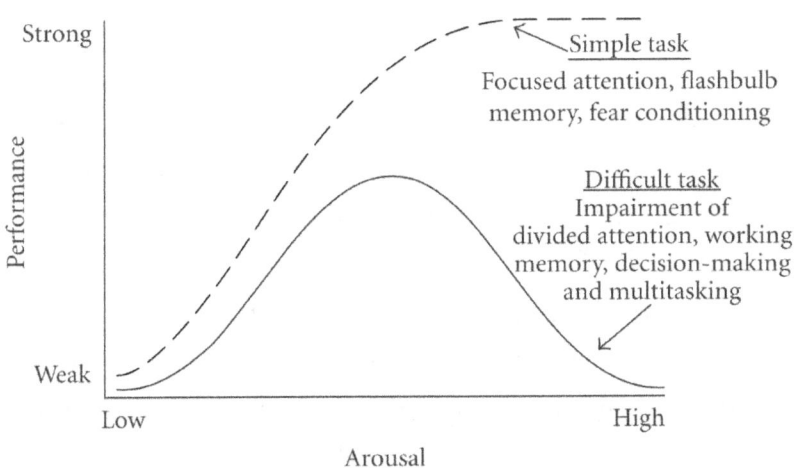

How to harness 'good stress' for success

While too much pressure can damage your performance and health in both the short-term and the long-term, we all need a certain amount of stress.

Life with no or little stress is probably a life of little meaning and purpose. The right amount of pressure takes you to that sweet spot where you perform to your potential. 'Eustress' is good stress that comes from positive challenges or exciting experiences.

Positive stress can also be a source of:
- determination
- motivation
- persistence
- endurance
- anticipation
- drive
- energy
- eagerness
- exhilaration

Think back to a successful first date, or when you gave an important presentation or competed in sport. You probably experienced some eustress that motivated you to do your best.

You'll be familiar with the physical symptoms of a stressful situation – racing heart, sweaty palms, butterflies in the tummy. Rather than noticing these symptoms with dread, you can choose to see them as signs that your body is preparing you to do well. It's making itself ready to rise to the challenge and succeed.

Types of recovery activities

If you're experiencing these symptoms of stress too often, it does take a toll. Reducing your baseline level of stress and making time for recovery is vital to protect your long-term ability to perform.

Sleep

When we're busy, sleep is often the first thing to go as we struggle to find more time. Of course, stress also interferes with our ability to get a good night's rest, while ironically, a good sleep is just what we need to better cope with stress.

Sleeplessness is linked to stress and the release of stress hormones, which severely affect the health of the cells. In fact, your cortisol levels mirror your circadian rhythms when functioning normally.

Circadian Rhythm – Stress Response

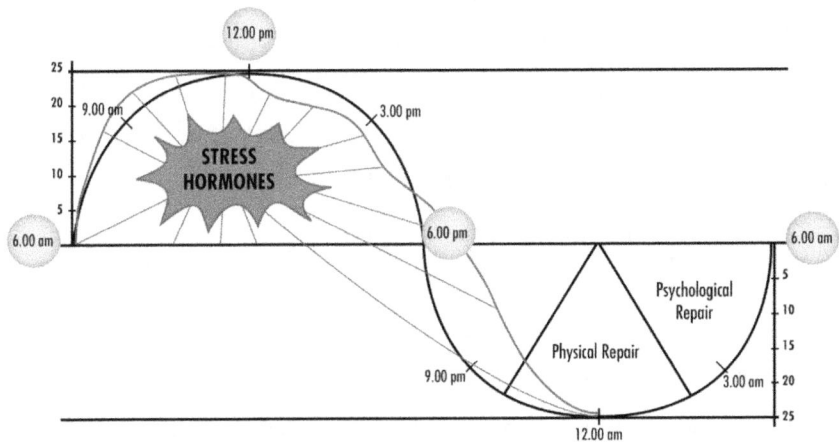

Normal Response

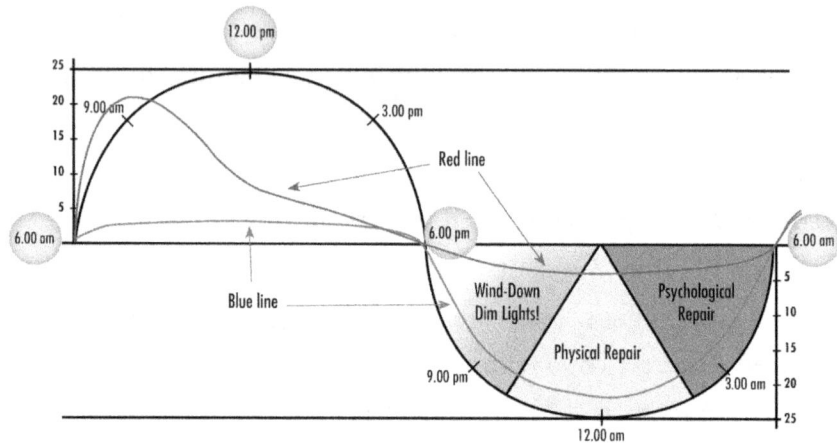

The red line shows a normal cortisol response during a normal day, mapped against the blue line of our repair hormones such as melatonin and growth hormone. Contrast that to the above with a chronic stress response, notice the elevated cortisol and complete lack of repair hormones.

Cortisol takes several hours to leave the body, so it is vitally important to wind down your day and begin reduce the stress inputs such as artificial light and poor stimulation for the mind such as watching TV (especially the news). Developing good afternoon/evening habits when you wind down and take time out for yourself becomes key.

Good quality sleep ensures that you are able to produce more of the repair hormones which will ensure you replenish your stress hormones which you will begin to use the next day, a lack of replenishment of these stress hormones can lead to adrenal fatigue which will put you flat on your back and unable to get out of bed with your body forcing you to stop completely or become ill, also forcing you back to bed.

Healthy sleep habits

Good sleep habits include things that train your body clock to go to sleep and wake up at the same time each day. Try to keep to a set bedtime, including on weekends.

If you have trouble falling asleep, try some meditation techniques or one of these other activities to support quality sleep:

- Take a bath
- Connect with the night sky
- Journal – empty the mind before sleep
- Make your to do list for the next day
- Essential oils to diffuse to help sleep e.g. lavender, roman chamomile, vetiver, bergamot
- Yoga
- Connect deeply with your partner

What to avoid:

- TV or other screens
- Caffeine
- Eating late
- Working too late
- Talking or arguing too late
- Reading too much (not in the 15 minutes leading to sleep)

This table offers substitutes for 'sleep detracting' activities with more sleep promoting ones

Rather than this ...	Try this ...
Reading/TV/eating etc in bed	Bed is ONLY for sleeping
Waking up or going to sleep at different times	Waking up or going to sleep at the same times
Thinking of what you have to do tomorrow	Plan the next days activities
Taking your problems to bed	Write out worries with a pen and paper
Exercising too soon before bed	Exercise regularly and earlier in the day
Having noise come into your room	Noise free bedroom
Being too hot or cold	Even and comfortable temperature

The power of light

Make sure you spend plenty of time in natural daylight during the day. Light is the most effective tool we have for influencing our circadian rhythms. In the same vein, make sure you limit exposure to bright lights and digital devices in the evenings. Our brains are particularly sensitive to the blue light waves from artificial light sources. If you have to keep using your laptop or phone, make sure you're using the night-time settings that give the screen an orange tone, so it emits less blue light. Also consider changing some of your light bulbs to a warmer bulb, or to colour-changing Wi-Fi-controlled bulbs. Use these warmer lights at night and set your brain up for sleep.

If you travel across time zones for work, light is your best weapon to beat jetlag. Use cleverly timed exposure to day light when you need to be awake, then avoid artificial light when you need to sleep.

If you consistently have trouble sleeping or rarely feel well-rested, or struggle with any of the other symptoms of burnout, talk to your GP.

Questions for you
1. I relax best by:
2. Sometimes my ideal night-time rest is hindered by:
3. My night bed-time routine will now include:

Take more daily mini breaks

Although tempting, it's counterproductive to ditch breaks when we're under the pump. It's vital to be disciplined about taking regular breaks during the day to recharge. Many top business people focus in chunks of time no longer than 40 minutes to an hour. You might stop for only five minutes but your brain (and your body) will be at their best for longer.

As well as frequent mini breaks, take time for a real lunch break whenever you can. This means stepping away from your desk and your devices. Even if it's short, your joints, your brain, your eyes need a change of scene and a chance to truly savour your food. Don't worry about lost productivity. Your subconscious brain will keep generating solutions to whatever problem you've been working on while you're eating your lunch.

After hours, make sure your time with friends and family is time where you are actually present with them. There's still no substitute for face-to-face connection for nurturing an important relationship.

Finally, stop to celebrate your wins. After completing a tough task, don't rush on to the next thing but pause to recognise what you've just achieved. As well as doing this with a tiny pat on the back each day, invest in more formal team celebrations every few months or so.

Mindfulness and meditation

With increasing work demands and the pressures of our go-go-go modern lives, it can be challenging to fully focus on the task at hand. Increasingly, we are thinking about work when we are home and home when we are at work. One solution is to cultivate the habit of mindfulness.

Mindfulness is such a popular topic nowadays, but what is it really? Put simply, it's deliberately bringing your attention to the present. It includes being calmly aware and accepting of your thoughts and feelings, without judgment.

Regularly training your brain in mindfulness can help you recover from stress and be more resilient. It also helps you improve the quality of your attention when you're working, and thereby improve the quality of your work.

There are countless mindfulness and meditation activities, but here are three to get you started.

Square breathing

How do I normally breathe?
Which hand is moving more? (select)

Chest hand / Tummy hand / Both

How many breaths do you take per minute? One breath = inhale + exhale

_____ bpm (breaths per minute)

How does this compare to the average number of breaths per minute? (select)

Slower / Fits into the average / Faster

How to breathe properly

Get comfortable. If you are sitting, put your feet flat on the floor and make sure your back is supported. If you are lying down, lie down flat on your back.

Notice your natural breathing. Put one hand on your chest, and the other on your stomach. Which hand is moving more? We want our stomach hand to be moving more than our chest hand.

Slow down your breathing. Start to breathe deeply and slowly. When you're ready, start pausing when your lungs are full, and again when your lungs are empty. Count to four for each stage of the breath. Repeat the square at least five times.

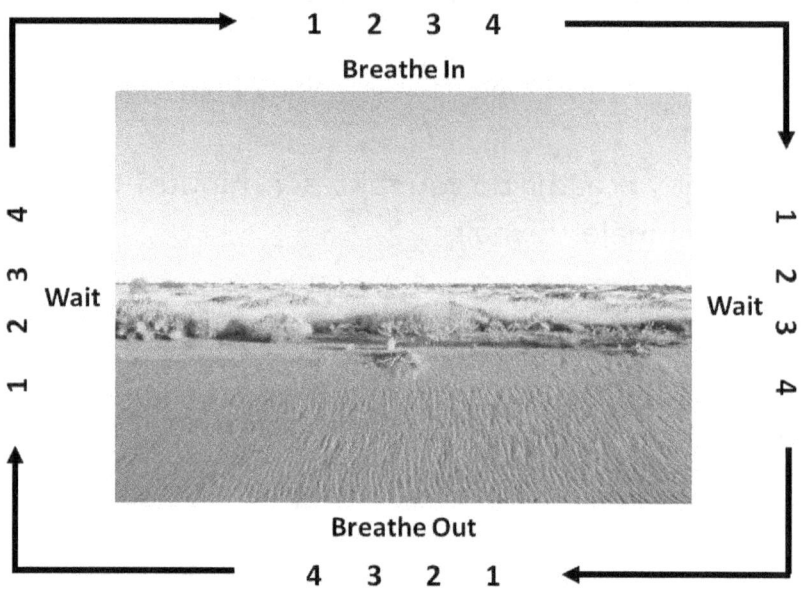

Body scan
Gradually become aware of each body part in turn, observing how it feels without any judgment. Starting at your toes, do you feel warmth, coolness, pressure, space, scratchiness, buzzing etc? Move on to your feet, then your ankles, and continue slowly. When you become aware you've lost concentration, just calmly bring your attention back without judgment.

Guided meditation
Find a guided meditation online, or in an app such as Headspace

or Calm. Or join a meditation class, or a yoga class. Yoga typically incorporates mindfulness throughout the physical poses as well as a meditation at the end of the class.

Mindfulness is simple, but it's not easy. However, with practice it does get easier, and it doesn't have to take long. On those days when your best intentions fly out the window and you really can't take a lunch break, just take two minutes. Even two minutes of square breathing in the lift could help get you through the day with more energy to perform.

Active recovery

When you finally get some spare time, it's tempting to just flop on the couch with a glass of wine. However, this isn't usually the most effective form of stress management. Better results come from active recreation that involves socialising with people, or doing something physical, or being in nature. Better still – see if you can combine all three!

Don't be afraid to think outside the square. One IT executive I was coaching felt his life had become very one-dimensional – work, work and more work. He was starting to experience the brain fog, low motivation and loss of energy that comes with burnout. When we talked about active recovery, he remembered he had been wanting to try geocaching. Geocaching is a fun outdoor activity where you use a GPS or a smartphone app to find 'treasure' hidden by other users. He loved the thrill of uncovering the hidden caches and it was something his adolescent kids were happy to join in with.

If you're struggling for ideas, what activities did you enjoy when you were younger? For some options, consider these active, social and/or outdoors activities:

- going for a walk, talk and coffee date
- organising a BBQ by the river
- taking the footy and a picnic to a park with friends or family
- inviting a friend to a music gig
- sending an open invitation to your friends and family to bring you along to more events and activities
- rock-climbing (indoors or out)
- stand-up paddle boarding
- kayaking
- bushwalking and hiking
- mountain biking
- yoga, boxing or gym classes
- martial arts courses
- team sports
- growing your own vegetables
- browsing sites that list upcoming events in your city for something that piques your interest

Make a note here – what are your favourite active recovery activities?

1.	
2.	
3.	

Emotional health

Whenever you feel a painful emotion, there are six steps you can quickly take to break limiting patterns, find the benefit of that emotion and set yourself up so that in the future, you can get the lesson from the emotion and eliminate the pain more quickly.

1 **Identify what you're really feeling.** Most people are so overloaded, they don't even know what they're feeling. Try to lower the intensity of what you are feeling using some of the relaxation techniques in this book, or simply taking a short walk outside. It makes it easier to learn from that emotion.

2 **Acknowledge and appreciate your emotions.** You never want to make your emotions wrong. Be thankful that your brain is sending you a signal of support – a call to action to

make a change in either your perception or in your actions. Cultivate the feeling of appreciation of *all* emotions. Whatever you resist tends to persist.

3 **Be curious about the message the emotion is offering you.**
Four questions to ask are:
What do I really want to feel?
What would I have to believe in order to feel the way I've been feeling?
What am I willing to do to create a solution and handle this right now?
What can I learn from this?

4 **Get confident!** The quickest and most powerful way to handle any emotion is to remember a time when you felt a similar emotion and realise that you've handled this emotion before. Ask yourself: what did I do then that was effective?

5 **Get certain you can handle this not only today, but the future as well.** Rehearse handling situations where this action signal would come up in the future. See, hear and feel yourself handling the situation easily.

6 **Get excited and take action.** Get excited that you can easily handle this emotion, and take some action right away to prove that you've handled it.

Common Thought/Feeling	Also felt through	Message	Solution
Discomfort	Boredom, impatience, unease, distress, mild embarrassment.	Something is not quite right. Maybe the way you're perceiving things is off, or the actions you're taking are not producing the results you want.	Clarify what you do want. Refine your actions – try a different approach. If not dealt with, it can lead to more intensified discomfort. 'The threat of attack is greater than the attack itself' is a common saying in martial arts. Your imagination can make things 100 times more intense than anything we could experience in real life.
Fear	Low levels of concern, apprehension to intense worry, anxiety, fright or even terror.	Fear is simply the anticipation that something that's going to happen soon needs to be prepared for. 'Be prepared'. We either need to cope with the situation or to do something to change it. Most people will try to deny their fear, or they wallow in it.	You don't want to surrender to fear and amplify it by starting to think the worst that could happen, nor do you want to pretend it's not there. What actions do you need to take to deal with the situation in the best possible way? Antidote to fear – you must make a decision to have faith.
Hurt	Feelings of hurt are usually generated by a sense of loss. When people are hurt – they often lash out at others.	The hurt signal is that we have an expectation that has not been met. Maybe someone didn't keep their word and you feel a loss of trust. Perhaps the sense of loss, is what creates the feeling of hurt.	Realise that in reality you may not have lost anything. Maybe what you need to lose is the false perception that this person is trying to wound or hurt you. Ask yourself, 'Is there really loss here'? Elegantly and appropriately communicate your feeling of loss to the person involved.

Common Thought/Feeling	Also felt through	Message	Solution
Anger	Feelings of being mildly irritated, to being angry, resentful, furious, or even enraged.	The message of anger is that an important rule or standard that you hold for your life has been violated by someone else — or maybe even by you.	Realise that you may have misinterpreted the situation completely, that your anger about this person breaking your rules may be based on the fact that they don't know what's most important to you. Realise that even if a person did violate one of your standards, your rules are not necessarily the right rules, even though you feel as strongly as you do about them. Ask yourself a more empowering question like, 'in the long run, is it true that this person really cares about me?' Interrupt the anger by asking yourself, 'What can I learn from this? How can I communicate the importance of these standards I hold for myself to this person in a way that causes them to want to help me, and not violate my standards again in the future?'

Common Thought/Feeling	Also felt through	Message	Solution
Frustration	When we feel like we're surrounded by roadblocks in our lives, where we are continuously putting out effort, but not receiving rewards, we tend to feel the emotion of frustration.	This is an exciting signal, as it means your brain believes you could be doing better than you currently are. It's different from disappointment, which is the feeling that there's something you want in your life but you'll never get it. It's a signal for you to become more flexible.	Realise that frustration is your friend, and brainstorm new ways to get a result. Get some input on how to deal with the situation. Find a role model, someone who has found a way to get what you want. Get fascinated by what you can learn that could help you handle this challenge not only today, but in the future.
Disappointment	Can be destructive if you don't deal with it quickly. It's the devastating feeling of being let down or that you're going to miss out on something forever. Anything that makes you feel sad or defeated as a result of expecting more than you get is disappointing.	The message disappointment offers you is that an expectation you have had is probably not going to happen, so it's time to change your expectations to make them more appropriate for this situation and take action to set and achieve a new goal immediately.	Immediately figure out something you can learn from this situation that could help you in the future to achieve the very thing you were after in the first place. Set a new inspiring goal to progress towards. Identify you may be judging too soon. 'God's delays are not God's denials'. Realise the situation is not over yet, and develop more patience. Completely re-evaluate what you want and start to develop an even more effective plan for achieving it. Cultivate an attitude of positive expectancy about what will happen in the future, regardless of what has happened in the past.

Common Thought/Feeling	Also felt through	Message	Solution
Guilt	Emotions of guilt, regret, remorse are among the emotions human beings do most to avoid in life – and this is valuable.	Guilt tells you that you have violated one of your own highest standards, and that you must do something immediately to ensure that you're not going to violate that standard again in the future. Guilt is the ultimate leverage for many people in changing a behaviour. Some people try to deal with their guilt by denying and suppressing it. However, it only comes back stronger. People can feel so remorseful about something they once did that they allow themselves to feel inferior for the rest of their lives.	Acknowledge that you have, in fact, violated a critical standard you hold for yourself. Absolutely commit yourself to making sure this behaviour will never happen again in the future. Rehearse in your mind now – if you could live it again, how would you deal with the same situation you feel guilty about in a way that is consistent with your own highest personal standards?

Common Thought/Feeling	Also felt through	Message	Solution
Inadequacy	A feeling of unworthiness occurs anytime we feel we can't do something we should be able to do.	It's not that you don't presently have a level of skill necessary for the task at hand. It's telling you that you need more information, understanding, strategies, tools or confidence.	Simply ask 'Is this really an appropriate emotion for me to feel in this situation?' 'Do I just need to change the way I am perceiving things?' Appreciate the encouragement to improve. Remind yourself that you're not perfect, and that you don't need to be. Find a role model, someone effective in the area in which you feel inadequate and get some coaching from them. When one feels inadequate, they tend to fall into the trap of learned helplessness, and they begin to see the problem as being a permanent one with themselves.

Common Thought/Feeling	Also felt through	Message	Solution
Overload or overwhelm	Grief, depression and helplessness are merely expressions of feeling overloaded or overwhelmed. If the problem appears too big, or outside their control – it can be perceived as permanent, pervasive and personal. People go into these emotional states whenever they perceive their world in a way that makes them feel like there's more going on than they can possibly deal with – pace, amount, or intensity of sensations seem overwhelming.	The message of being overwhelmed is that you need to re-evaluate what's most important to you in this situation. The reason you're overloaded is that you need to revaluate what's most important to you in this situation. The reason you are overloaded is that you're trying to deal with too many things at once, and you're trying to change everything overnight.	Decide, out of all the things you're dealing with in your life, what the absolute most important thing is for you to focus on. Write down all the things that are most important for you to accomplish and put them in an order of priority. Just putting them down on paper will allow you to begin to feel a sense of control over what is going on. Tackle the first thing on your list and continue to take action until you've mastered it. You will soon build momentum and let your brain know that the problem is not permanent, and that you can always come up with a solution. When you feel that it's appropriate to start letting go of an overwhelming emotion like grief, start focusing on what you can control and realise that there must be some empowering meaning to it all, even though you can't comprehend it yet. Focus on something that you can control and deal with things one step at a time.

Common Thought/Feeling	Also felt through	Message	Solution
Loneliness	Anything that makes us feel alone, apart, or separate from others belongs in this category.	You need a connection with people.	Realise that you can reach out and make a connection immediately and end the loneliness. Identify what kind of connection you do need. Remind yourself that being lonely means that you really care about people, and you love to be with them. You need to find out what kind of connection you need with somebody right now, and then take an action immediately to make that happen.

How Peter learned to beat burn-out

Peter Lopez, aged 42, is a hard-working tech entrepreneur. He loves his work and had been putting in long hours seven days a week. His evenings were often spent networking for the sake of his business. He was always multitasking and surviving on very little sleep each night. Peter felt this full-on approach had always been part of his DNA.

To Peter, it was normal to wake up with his phone or laptop in the bed or on the floor beside him, or even to fall asleep on the couch while working. As well as this poor sleep hygiene, Peter allowed very little time for recovery – he saw it as a non-productive use of time. To cope, he drank copious amounts of coffee.

Peter has always prided himself on his attention to detail while working under constant pressure to meet deadlines, and still having an active social life. Unfortunately, over the 12 months before I started coaching Peter, the qualities he had always thought of as his signature strengths – his drive, high performance and attention to detail – had started slipping away. Clients were now having to chase him up about uncompleted or inaccurate work. Close friends and work mates admitted he was coming across as disengaged and uninterested. Peter himself acknowledged he didn't have the energy or the enthusiasm that he previously had, and he felt stressed and burnt out.

Before implementing any programs, we ran a number of assessments to measure Peter's levels of stress, sleep quality and energy expenditure over several days. The results were persuasive for Peter to make changes, and we also suggested he check in with his GP. It showed his stress levels were through the roof, with virtually no recovery periods. Peter's sleep patterns were patchy at best, and showed broken sleep with insufficient recovery or repair to his body. At the same time, Peter had already started running 12 km a week to try to reduce his stress and anxiety.

We developed a recovery program that included various tools such as stress-relieving breathing techniques and meditation. I advised Peter to stop running for the time being because that was exacerbating his levels of stress, and replaced it with mindful walking.

He also agreed to forego any technology, TV or work-related activities during the hour before bedtime. Instead, he made the time to read books again and to re-engage with his hobbies of furniture-restoration and trivia nights.

Within three weeks, Peter was already seeing a clear improvement in how he was feeling and thinking. Despite setting aside more time for recovery activities, Peter felt more in control of his workload than before, and started each day with greater energy and focus. A friend commented on how pleased he was to see Peter back to his usual positive, enthusiastic self.

When you don't have time to relax

If you can't find time in your schedule for recovery, first consider where you can save time. Remember that often when you say, 'I don't have time,' you're really saying, 'It's not a priority.'

When it comes to time management, there are countless books and courses available. No doubt you've got a few favourite tricks already. We won't go into time management processes here, but to put time-management in the bigger picture of work-life agility, you must be guided by your personal purpose and values. Remind yourself what's 'mission critical' to you personally, and what the strategic priorities of your work are. This helps you decide how to divvy up your limited time between competing demands. It makes it easier to say no to people wanting to load up your to-do list if the work they're suggesting isn't aligned with your strategic priorities. Then, it's a matter of setting and reinforcing your boundaries – an area of self-development for many people.

If you're still struggling to allocate time to recovery activities, ask yourself these powerful questions:

1. What will your life look like when you're 60 if you continue your current work habits and stress levels? Imagine you're there now. What is your health like in the future? How strong is your marriage, your friendships, and your relationships your children? How satisfied are you with your life?
2. Think of someone at work who is older than you and known as a workaholic. How satisfied do you think they are with their life? How is their health, the quality of their relationships, etc?
3. If you were able to hear what is said about you in your eulogy, what do you think people would say? What would you *like* to hear them say?
4. To sustain the vitality to achieve your goals and purpose, do you need to spend more, less or the same amount of time on proactive recovery activities?

There's never been a better time than now to create the lifestyle that will change your future.

CHAPTER 6: HEALTHY WORKING RELATIONSHIPS

In most workplaces, we don't get to choose our colleagues, clients and superiors. If we're lucky, we do make some long-term work friends, but there will always be others we don't click with. Add to that the increasing pressure we face in the business world, and the importance to our identities of succeeding at work. It's no surprise we sometimes lose our cool. However, we need to find ways to manage frustration, anger and conflict, for the sake of our health and our careers.

Manage frustration and save your health

Anger is common and normal, but your responses to it can put your health and career at risk. Each angry outburst affects your body. Anger is not just something that happens in your brain, it causes physical effects too. When you feel angry, some of the common short-term effects are:

- changes in the level of hormones such as cortisol, testosterone and adrenaline
- higher blood pressure
- headache
- insomnia
- indigestion

If you're prone to angry outbursts, the risks keep accumulating throughout the day. Over time, frequent anger can lead to:
- more wear and tear on your heart
- stroke
- heart attack
- depression and anxiety

As well as these worrying physical effects, feeling angry can interfere with your performance. You can have trouble concentrating and achieving your goals. You might feel embarrassed about losing control, and come across as immature, difficult or not suitable for promotion.

Anger itself is not the problem

It's good to remember that there is nothing wrong with feeling angry from time to time. Anger is no less justified than any other emotion. We all experience a range of emotions every day, from regret to contentment to pride to disappointment, and many more in between. Anger is just another of those feelings.

Frustration and anger are warning signs designed to let you know something is undesirable or unacceptable to you. It's what you do with your anger, not the anger itself, that has the greatest consequences.

What are we to do with anger?

Our society often cultivates us to believe that anger is a negative and unhelpful emotional experience. Many of us have learned to avoid difficult conversations and bottle up our frustrations to keep the peace ... at least until those frustrations overflow. Ironically, the more you try to hold in your emotions, the more likely it is that they will overflow in an uncontrolled and destructive way. Alternatively, if you do allow yourself to fly off the handle, you're giving yourself permission to stay angry and get even angrier.

Are you guilty of leaving your frustrations unaddressed until they build up and become unmanageable? For example, maybe your boss at work has been taking the credit for a highly successful project and neglecting to mention the key role you played in it. To avoid conflict with your boss, you bottle it up and don't say anything just yet. Then, on the train home you're dying to sit down but a young guy pushes you out of the way for the last seat. Finally, when you arrive home, you discover your partner has forgotten you planned to see a movie together and is halfway out the door to the gym instead. You overreact when telling them in no uncertain terms how annoyed you are with their thoughtlessness, and even slam the door behind them.

Anger management begins with self-awareness

If you get too worked up, you can't think properly to communicate, problem-solve or negotiate. You revert to more basic, animal ways of reacting. You won't be able to deal with the situation in a mature way. This is why we have the saying, 'Revenge is a dish best served cold.' However, if you can calm yourself down *before* you get too worked up, you can do something rational about the problem.

The first step towards anger management is becoming aware of how your body reacts. Often, our body sends out warning signals before the thought, 'I'm getting really angry' even comes to mind. Some common precursors include:

- headaches
- gritting your teeth
- repetitive and negative thoughts
- holding your breath
- muscle tension
- tension in your tone of voice
- feeling hot and sweaty.

Be proactive, not reactive

If you start to notice these physical signs, before you get out of control, do something to keep your cool.

Take five

When you can feel your temperature rising, take a break. Go for a walk, get some fresh air, take an early lunch break or make a cup of tea. Use any excuse to get you out of there even if it's faking an urgent need for the loo, saying 'Can you give me two minutes? I'm dying for a drink of water.' During your break, take a few slow, deep breaths until you feel your body relax. Temporarily removing yourself from the situation and doing something different will help you come back with a cooler head and a fresh viewpoint.

Label and accept the emotion

You might say to yourself something like, 'I am experiencing the feeling of anger. This feeling will pass. It's OK to feel angry, but I want to act in line with my values.' Practise self-compassion, which we discussed in the chapter on mindset.

Gain perspective

Ask yourself what it is that's really upsetting you. What seems to be the problem on the surface might be hiding a deeper concern.

Consider whether your expectations or your interpretation of the situation might be contributing to your anger. Perhaps your employee is simply too inexperienced to have realised they were making a public gaffe (you have unrealistic expectations). Perhaps your partner isn't late to your date because they don't care about you, but because traffic was particularly bad (inaccurate interpretation).

Also transport yourself to the future and ask yourself, 'Will this still matter in a year from today? In a month? Tomorrow?' Typically, it won't.

Listen

When communication becomes frustrating, we have a nasty habit of spending our listening time a) formulating our next response, and b) looking for a gap in the conversation to interject. Chances are that the other person is feeling unheard, and also becoming more frustrated.

Work hard to listen to, not just hear, the other side of it. Acknowledge the other person's position before bringing up your own. If you need more time to convey your point, organising and setting aside another time to discuss it may be the way to go.

Expend that energy

Because anger taps into and activates the sympathetic nervous system, it can really be classed in terms of energy. You can probably feel this in your body when you're angry. Our descriptions reflect this too: feeling like a pressure cooker, getting riled up, boiling over. Some people find it helpful to expend this pent-up energy in productive ways. Going for a run, joining a sports team or attending a boxing class are a couple of the ideas that can help.

Learn to relax around the clock

It seems obvious but achieving a state of relaxation needs as much practice as any other skill. Each time you relax and enjoy yourself, the pathways in the brain responsible for this are reinforced, and you are more likely to be able to replicate the feeling. Plus, when you start the day with a lower baseline level of stress and tension, you can better cope with the inevitable stresses of the day. This is why relaxation skills are not just for the moment but impact your mood over a variety of contexts. Find what works for you. There are plenty of ideas in the chapter on recovery and resilience.

How Rachael kept her cool

Rachael was 29 years old and the second-in-charge of a small bank's client relations department. Unfortunately, she rarely saw eye-to-eye with her boss. He seemed to get away with doing as little work as possible. He did just enough to 'cover his butt' and expected her to work well beyond her pay grade. What's more, she found him patronising, and old-fashioned in his attitudes.

She tried to keep her cool but had recently embarrassed herself by rudely snapping at him in a meeting with more senior managers. Also, when Rachael met with her boss in his office, team members on the other side of the floor often heard her raised voice. Although she felt justified in her irritation and anger, she also felt embarrassed at her immature responses.

Rachael started observing the physical signs that she was at risk of losing her temper. For her, it was muscle tension, especially in her shoulders and face. She decided to implement the simple strategy of excusing herself. At home, she practised saying things like, 'I'd like to pause there and pick up this conversation later,' or 'Excuse me, I'm expecting a phone call. I'll follow up by email afterwards.' In her own office, she would then take a few deep breaths, and reflect on what it was that was really upsetting her. (Was it indeed the results of the latest customer survey, or was it because her boss failed to acknowledge how hard she had worked on it?) With a bit of perspective, she was able to return to the conversation with a more constructive attitude.

Self-assessment – responding to anger

What are the things most likely to trigger *your* anger?
- Rejection
- Discrimination
- Being late
- Disrespect
- Inefficiency
- Rude behaviour
- Lack of appreciation
- Laziness
- Selfishness
- Incompetence
- Unfair treatment
- Being let down
- Criticism
- Something else.

What are some strategies you have successfully used in the past to stay cool when you felt yourself getting angry?

Resolving conflict at work

One of the things that can make us feel stressed and angry at work is conflict with other people. Conflict is not just uncomfortable but bad news for business.

One study involving workers in nine countries found an overwhelming 85% of people experience conflict at work. It also found that dealing with workplace conflict takes up 2.8 hours a week on average. Not to mention the poorer performance and increased absenteeism and turnover that can result.

It can be tempting to try to avoid all conflict. But the secret to conflict management is *not* to try and eliminate all disagreements from the workplace.

Conflict is inevitable and necessary

Just like anger, not only is conflict inevitable, it's necessary. When a workplace has zero conflict, that's likely a sign that people are disengaged and lack passion. Change and innovation don't happen without disagreements. When we feel strongly about our work, clashes are bound to happen. It follows that the most successful businesses are those which handle conflict constructively.

What does constructive conflict look like?
Address it early and objectively
For starters, don't let disputes fester. Address the issue sooner rather than later. It's a good idea to set aside a meeting time. When you meet, describe the problem objectively rather than using loaded,

emotional language. This only makes the other person feel defensive and respond in kind.

For example, instead of saying, 'When you're late in the mornings, I have to pick up your slack. You need to get more organised because the work is suffering,' try to be more objective. 'I'm finding that I don't have enough time in the mornings to get everything done when it's only me here. Can we work something out together?'

Practise your best listening

Next, make sure you're listening carefully. There is always another side to the story. We simply don't know what we don't know. It is human nature to put a halo above our own heads yet view the other person critically for the exact same behaviours. It's helpful to keep an open mind about the "facts" that may in fact be mere assumptions that we are making.

For example, you might criticise a co-worker for being disorganised and arriving late to an important meeting. Meanwhile, if you were running late in the morning, you wouldn't label yourself as disorganised, you'd know you were late because you forgot to leave time to ring your mum for her birthday.

Look for common ground

While you're listening, try to find some common ground. It might be the reason that you both feel so strongly about the same issue. Sometimes you both want the same outcome but see different ways to get there. At least look for some small part of the other person's argument that you agree with. This will instantly defuse tension and re-establish some rapport so you can keep working towards a win–win solution.

Aim for a win–win solution

To find this win–win outcome, you need to know what both parties want. Also make it clear what you are looking for. Sometimes, both people might need to concede a bit to reach this mutually satisfying result.

Let's say you and your boss have different ideas about how much supervision you need. On one hand, you feel they are micromanaging you at every step throughout the day. On the other hand, they feel they have to check your work closely because it's their job. You might come to a win–win agreement where they agree not to check on your progress every day. In return, you'll send them a short update each afternoon, and give them a detailed rundown every Monday morning.

Address the negative emotions

Once a common agreement has been reached, it's then possible to address the negative feelings. If you don't have an agreement yet, each person will still feel defensive and this will be difficult. If you skip this step, the negative emotions will continue to fester and probably cause further arguments down the track. There's no doubt talking about your feelings can be uncomfortable, but it can save you future headaches.

For example, you could say, 'Thank you for taking the time to talk about this. I felt like you didn't have any faith in my ability to do the job, and part of me worried that you were right. I'm looking forward to proving I can do the work with more independence.' Invite the other person to address their own negative emotions and bring an open mind to what they have to say. As Winston Churchill said, 'Courage is what it takes to stand up and speak. Courage is also what it takes to sit down and listen.'

CHAPTER 7: THE ANTIDOTE TO PROLONGED SITTING

You've probably heard that 'sitting is the new smoking'. In our modern lives we spend an awful lot of time on our backsides and it's making us unwell. Have you ever stopped to add up how long you spend sitting down? Not just in the office, but on your commute, on business travel, when you're relaxing at home, and even when you're catching up with friends. It all adds up.

To protect your vitality from the costs of prolonged sitting, the best medicine is to keep moving throughout the day.

What do long periods of sitting do to your body?

It was back in the 1950s that we started to suspect that prolonged sitting was dangerous to our health. Researchers found London bus drivers were twice as likely to have heart attacks as the conductors. While the drivers were sitting all day, the bus conductors were moving around to collect fares and help passengers on and off the bus.

A rapidly growing body of scientific evidence now shows a variety of dangers of consistently sitting for long periods. They range from merely uncomfortable conditions to seriously fatal ones.

Tight hips and weak muscles

Spending hours in a seated position causes the muscles at the front of your hip, your hip flexors, to tighten and shorten. This has flow-on effects on your posture and movement. At the same time, the gluteal muscles at the back of your hips, in your backside, get weak from being elongated and not exercised. Weak glute muscles can reduce your overall balance and fitness.

Back pain

Sitting is not your spine's favourite position and it can start to complain with aches and pains, especially when you have tight hip flexors.

Neck and shoulder tension

Sitting at a desk, using a keyboard and mouse and staring a screen all place a strain on your neck, shoulders and upper back. Staying in the same position for long periods will create tight, sore muscles and joints.

Varicose veins and DVTs

When blood pools in your legs because you've been sitting for too long, the effects add up over time. It can lead to uncomfortable and visible varicose veins, or deep vein thrombosis (DVT). DVTs are a blood clot in your vein, which can travel to other parts of your body and create life-threatening blockages.

Diabetes

Sitting increases your blood-sugar levels and your insulin resistance. Eventually, it can lead to diabetes. In fact, people who spend more time sitting have a 112 per cent higher risk of developing diabetes.

Heart disease

The longer you spend sitting, the higher your chances of having a heart disease or stroke. For example, one study found that men who watched more than 3.3 hours of TV a day (on average) had a 64% higher chance of dying from cardiovascular disease than those who watched only 1.5 hours a day.

Cancer

Your risk of some types of cancer, including lung, uterine, and colon cancers, seems to be greater when you spend more time sitting.

Poorer mental health

Research tells us that anxiety and depression is more common in people who sit around more. We don't yet know exactly why, but we do know that exercise helps boost mood. Staying active in small ways every half hour could help to maintain a positive mood all day.

Why you need short breaks, often

The good news? Research has shown that regardless of how long you sit in total, regularly moving around throughout the day can reduce the dangers of sitting. Broadly speaking, there are two categories of physical activity:

- Incidental physical activity, also known as activities of daily living. These include walking up stairs or to the cafe, household chores, and running errands. Combined, they accumulate to a fair chunk of time.
- Structured physical activity, which we covered in the chapter on exercise. This is continuous activity, lasting more than ten minutes, which uses large muscle groups.

Both types of activity are necessary to maintain your vitality and quality of life. Vigorous exercise is great for your health but it's not enough to avoid the risks of prolonged sitting. So you already ran 10 km this morning? That's excellent, but it's still imperative to break up the rest of the day with plenty of incidental movement.

How to reduce the risks of prolonged sitting at work

You don't have to take long breaks to stand up and walk around, just frequent pauses. Aim for a ratio of two minutes of standing or walking for every 30 minutes of sitting. For example, when I'm on the phone, you'll rarely see me sitting down. I like to get up and walk around while talking.

Here are some more practical ideas to add bite-sized chunks of movement to your day in the office:
- Set a 30-minute timer on your phone to prompt you to stand up
- Use wearable technology that monitors your movement (such as a smart watch) to nudge you when you've been stationary for too long
- Get a standing desk and switch regularly between sitting and standing
- If you're in charge of a long meeting, incorporate short breaks for everyone to stand and stretch
- Walk to a colleague's desk rather than emailing them
- Print to your furthest printer
- Drink plenty of water during the workday to make sure you take regular walks to the loo
- Find a space to do a few stretches, body weight exercises or yoga movements

Stretching at your desk

There are plenty of simple stretches that you can easily do without leaving the office. Spending a long time in a fixed position or doing the same movements over again are the worst enemies of tight or aching muscles and joints. These stretches will help you feel more comfortable and maintain better posture over time.

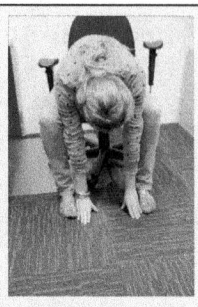 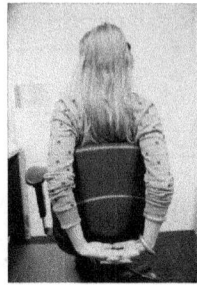 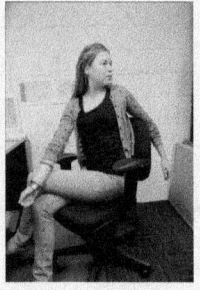 

The rock: Back Stretch

Sit towards the edge of your seat with your feet planted firmly on the floor.

Tuck your chin into your chest.

Gently lower your hands towards the floor.

This stretch should be felt in your back.

Hold for 20 seconds

Repeat 2–3 times

Chest opener:

Interlock fingers behind back. Slowly turn elbows inwards while straightening arms.

Good for slumped postures.

Hold for 10 secs

Repeat often

Spinal twist:

Sit with leg bent over the right, resting elbow of right arm on the outside of the left leg.

Apply pressure to the right and look over left shoulder.

Rear shoulder stretch:

Hold left elbow with right hand, then gently pull elbow behind head until tension is felt in shoulder.

Hold for 10 secs

Repeat both sides

Tricep stretch:

Hold the left arm above the elbow with right hand and gently pull to opposite shoulder as you look over the left.

Hold for 10 secs

Repeat both sides

Rear neck stretch:

Gentle tilt head forward until you feel a stretch at the back of your neck.

Hold for 5–10 secs

Repeat 2–3 times

Neck rotation:

Whilst sitting stable, turn head to look over left shoulder, feeling tension.

Repeat for right

Hold tension for 10 secs

Repeat 2–3 times

Side neck stretch:

Start with head in a comfortable position. Slowly tilt to the left side.

Hold for 10 secs

Don't over stretch do same on the right

Repeat 2–3 times

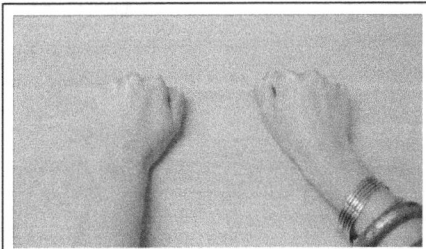 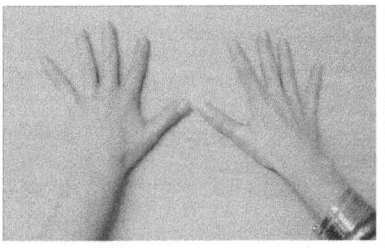

Separate and stretch fingers maximally. Hold for 10 secs. Relax, then bend fingers at knuckles for 10 secs. Repeat 2–3 times

  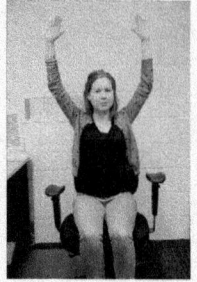

Chest stretch:

Interlock fingers behind neck. Pull shoulder blades together to create tension in upper back.

Hold tension for 10 secs. Relax

Repeat 2–3 times

Shoulder shrug:

Raise shoulders to ears until you feel slight tension.

Hold for 5 secs

Relax in normal position

Repeat 2–3 times.

Reach for the sky: Upper body stretch

Sit with feet planted firmly on floor.

Ensure head and back are upright.

Raise both hands above your head.

Reach up towards the ceiling, as high as possible until you feel a stretch in your entire upper body.

Hold for 20 seconds, repeat 2–3 times

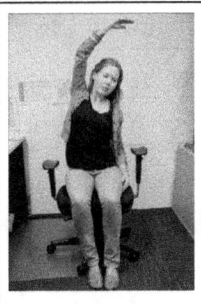 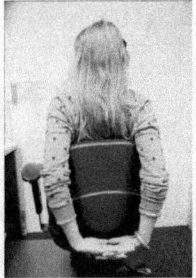  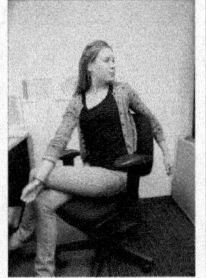

The Banana: Side Stretch

Sit with feet planted firmly on floor.

Ensure head and back are upright.

Raise one arm above your head, and the other alongside your body.

Slide the lowered arm down, this should create a long and short side of your body.

Create an arc with the raised arm, this stretch should be felt in the muscles on your longest side.

Hold for 20 seconds, repeat two times on each side.

The Emu: Shoulder Retraction

Sit towards the edge of your seat with your feet planted firmly on the floor.

Ensure head and back are upright.

Place hands together behind your lower back.

Pull shoulders back and down.

Hold for 20 seconds, repeat two times.

The Yes and No: Neck Stretch

Sit with feet planted firmly on floor.

Ensure head and back are upright.

Turn head towards your left shoulder.

Hold for 20 seconds, repeat two times on each side.

Lift chin up towards the ceiling.

Hold for 20 seconds, repeat two times and again with your chin lowered towards your chest.

The Twister: Lower Back Stretch

Sit with feet planted firmly on the floor.

Ensure head and back are upright.

Gently rotate your upper body towards your left, turning your head with you as you go.

This stretch should be felt in your back and sides.

Hold each stretch for 20 seconds, repeat two times on each side.

How to set up your workstation

When was the last time you checked your desk set up? If something is out of kilter and it's causing discomfort, you can't perform at your best.

To avoid the aches, pains and stiffness that come from working at a desk, it's important to set up your workstation to suit your individual body and the way you work. Run through this checklist and have a healthcare professional check your set up.

Chair

- Check the height of your chair. Are your thighs parallel to the floor? Adjust your chair so they are.
- Do your feet rest flat on the floor? If not, you may need to use a footrest.
- Check the height of your back rest. Adjust the back rest so the lumbar support fits into the small of your back and supports your spine.
- Check your back rest angle. Adjust it so that you are sitting upright, not leaning back.

Desk

- Check that your forearms are horizontal or sloping slightly towards the desk. Are your elbows just above the height of the desk?
- Adjust the height of either your desk or your chair to achieve this.

Footrest

- Now you have your chair at the correct height, check again whether your feet rest flat on the floor or whether you need a footrest.
- If you need a footrest, choose one that's large enough to fully support both feet.

Computer screen

- Check the position of your monitor on the desk. When you reach your arm out straight in front of you, your screen (or screens) should be about one arms' length away.
- Adjust the height of the monitor so that the top of the screen is below your eye level, and the centre of the screen is at your shoulder height.
- Make sure you don't have to bend your neck up and down too much to see the top and bottom of the screen.
- Keeping the screen clean with a regular wipe over helps to avoid eye strain.
- When you're using a laptop, using a docking station (and separate monitor, keyboard and mouse) can help achieve the ideal set up.

Keyboard and Mouse

- Check that you have room on the desk in front of the keyboard to rest the heel of your hands when you pause while typing.

- Check that there is a straight, relaxed line from your forearms to your hands. Adjust the slope of your keyboard if you need to.
- Is the mouse as close to you as possible? Having it too far to the side can create a sore shoulder. To give your dominant side a break, you can even practise using the mouse with your other hand.

Lighting

- Too much or too little light can cause eye strain and headaches.
- The ideal position for lighting in the workplace is to have lights running either side of the workstations, not directly overhead.
- If your desk is near a window, consider moving away from it. If that's not possible, turn your desk so neither you nor your screen face the window.

Glare and reflection

- Glare and reflection can also cause eye strain and other discomfort.
- You can check your screen by looking for glare and reflection when it's turned off.
- Then, with it turned on, block the light coming from a window or other light source with a piece of paper and see if that makes it easier to read the screen.

- You can remove reflection and glare by tilting the screen, using a light diffusing cover, and using blinds or window coverings.

Changing position and resting your eyes

Even a perfect workstation setup can create headaches, sore necks, shoulder pain and stiff spines when you stay in the same position without a break. When you're working at your computer you also need to rest your eyes frequently.

- Use the strategies in this chapter to get up and move around whenever you're at your desk. Remember, **every 30 minutes, take a two-minute break.**
- Every 15 minutes or so, refocus your eyes on a distant object for at least five seconds, or close your eyes and allow the muscles to completely relax.

Ergonomics outside the office

Many of us now spend hours working on our laptops and other mobile devices outside office hours, while travelling for work or while commuting. Remember that the same principles to prevent discomfort apply, no matter where you are.

Adjust your position to avoid muscle and joint strain. Use the checklist to adjust your set up when you work at a hot desk, or in a hotel room or airport lounge.

Also be mindful of how you use your smartphone. For example, don't slouch over your phone, but hold it up between your chest and your eyes. From time to time, put it down on a flat surface to type or text using your fingers.

Most importantly, keep taking those short, frequent breaks to move around and stretch.

How to hold walking meetings

Want to get more incidental activity into your day, inspire your colleagues to do the same and save time with a shorter meeting? It may be time to try a walking meeting.

First, scope out your route. Figure out an interesting path you could take that would see you back at the office in half an hour. You could also identify a shorter route with a park bench on the way, to take a break from walking.

Walking meetings are best for one-on-ones. It can be hard to talk with a large group of people while you're walking. You have two options for inviting your colleague to a walking meeting. You can ask them ahead of time to walk while you talk. This is helpful if they need to wear comfortable shoes or send you documents beforehand. Or you can ask them on the day, being prepared to stick to the meeting room if they're not up for it.

As you might have realised, it is harder to take notes while you're walking. If you stop at a park bench, take some notes then. Otherwise just jot down the actions as soon as you get back to your desk.

What about standing desks?

In the last ten years, standing desks have become much more readily available. But are they the solution to the wellbeing costs of too much time in the office? They can certainly help you change position so you're not sitting all the time. Some people find they improve their muscle and joint aches caused by sitting.

Look for one that's easy to move up and down, otherwise you won't use it. Also think about your footwear – standing in high heels could do your health more damage than good. When you stand, make sure the desk is at the right height to avoid strain on your shoulders from holding your arms up.

The key to getting the benefits of a standing desk is to regularly change your posture, not to stand for as long as possible. Standing still has many of the same consequences for your health as sitting still. So, perhaps you sit for half an hour, walk to the water cooler, sit for 20 minutes, then stand for 15 minutes.

Remember to check that your ergonomic set up still works when you're standing. When you stand up, reassess the position of your monitor, keyboard and mouse using the checklist above.

Flying and sitting

When you're travelling for work, there are some particular habits that help keep your body moving:
- Follow the DVT-prevention guide in the seat pocket in front of you and do those foot pumps and the other movements.

- Always get the aisle seat so you can easily stroll down the aisle every now and again.
- Don't sit down at your gate until you have to. Wander the airport for a little longer.
- Don't rush to board the plane first – it just means more sitting time.
- As soon as you check into your hotel, take a stroll around the neighbourhood.

Breaking up your sitting time after-hours

What about prolonged sitting in your home life? If you're tempted to just flop on the couch after a stressful day, I get it. However, even when you're watching TV, it's a great idea to stand up and stretch every half hour. Binge-watching a 30-minute TV series? What a perfect opportunity to get up and grab a glass of water between episodes.

When meeting up with friends or family, remember to think about incorporating some movement into your get-together. For example, stay on your feet at a BBQ instead of moulding yourself into a chair. Meet at the beach instead of a bar. Consider fun active outings like mini-golf, bowling, dancing or bushwalking instead of the movies or dinner. If you're needing to keep your distances from others due to health reasons, you can picnic in a quiet, spacious area and take a ball to kick around. Or have an extended family dance off over a video call, and show the kids the 'oldies' best moves.

In my own family, we make a point of stepping away from the screens on the weekend and taking a soccer ball to the park. My boys need to stretch their legs just as much as I do.

Exercises that counteract sitting

While any change of position is good for you when you've been sitting for a while, these targeted moves are especially helpful. Whether at work or at home, they provide an effective antidote to some of the effects of sitting.

Take a minute to do one of these exercises every time your 30-minute alarm goes off.

- Release right hip flexors by kneeling on one knee, with your other foot in front, under your other knee, and pushing your hips forward.
- Strengthen weak glute muscles with squats or lunges, focusing on squeezing your backside muscles as you push up.
- Stretch open your tight chest and shoulders by clasping your hands behind your back, pulling them down and back.
- Loosen tight neck muscles by dropping your head to one side and gently letting it roll it forward, down and around to the other shoulder, then back.
- Take yoga poses like downward-facing dog and forward fold to help your spine decompress.

A trainer or physiotherapist can help with correct technique and show you many more stretches to suit your particular needs. If the ideas in this chapter don't improve your aches and pains, ask a health professional for advice.

How Barry said goodbye to his neck pain and headaches

Chief Finance Officer Barry was 51 years old and suffering chronic pain when we began working together.

Barry is a former rugby and golf player. Unfortunately, due to injuries in his previous sports, sitting for long periods at work was causing him terrible pain. As well as chronic headaches, he experienced back and neck pain. He was spending a small fortune at the physiotherapist and was also taking heavy pain medication. These meds sometimes left him fatigued, drowsy and interfered with his sleep quality. The pain was affecting Barry's work productivity, seeing him take frequent sick leave. At home, he was often irritable and short with his wife and teenaged children.

We ordered an ergonomic chair and adjustable standing desk and made sure his set up was right for his body. We developed a desk stretching program which included standing and moving every 45 mins. I also coached Barry through introducing walking meetings to his team.

Outside work, I strongly recommended he do Pilates or yoga, which he is now committed to doing several times a week. He is also careful to limit the time he spends sitting watching TV or responding to emails when he gets home.

The results, in Barry's words, have been 'absolutely life changing'. He only occasionally needs to take pain medication. He doesn't need to see his physio as often. With less pain, he can now get seven hours of unbroken sleep a night. His productivity is back to where it should be, and he has only taken two days off in the last 12 months. He is even back playing golf.

CHAPTER 8: HEALTH CHECKS AT EVERY AGE

If you've started applying even a fraction of the strategies in this book to proactively cultivate your wellbeing and vitality, you are well on your way to work–life agility. Well done!

You can continue this proactive approach by getting the health checks you need at each stage of life. All of us need to periodically see our health professionals to monitor our physical health. Getting an early heads-up on any medical conditions you have lets you nip them in the bud and reduce their impact on your performance.

Talk to your GP about which tests are most relevant to you, and whether you need them more or less frequently than the average person.

In your 20s: Carefree

Health check	Why	How often
Skin check	To pick up skin cancers early so they can be treated and cured. Melanoma is the most common cancer in young Australian adults, aged 15–29 years. It accounts for more than 25% of all cancers in this age group.	Do a self-check every three months. If anything looks unusual, see your GP. In addition, see your GP for an annual skin check (or more often if needed).
Manage nutrition & alcohol consumption	Having a dietitian review your usual eating habits can make sure you're eating to fuel your health and performance, as well as catering to your unique needs.	If your health or usual dietary habits change (e.g. if you are diagnosed with coeliac disease, or decide to lose weight).
Vaccinations	HPV: The HPV vaccine (for both men and women) prevents the specific types of HPV that cause almost all cervical cancers. Flu: The flu is not a cold. Every year it causes hospitalisation and even death; in 2017, there were 1,255 deaths caused by flu in Australia. Travel: When you travel overseas you may be exposed to diseases that are preventable with immunisation.	If you did not have the HPV vaccine as a teenager, you can get it now. It involves two injections, 6–12 months apart. The flu vaccine is updated each year to protect against the strains most likely to be circulating in the coming flu season. Before you travel overseas, check with your doctor if you're due for any vaccinations.

Health check	Why	How often
Sexual health check	Most sexually transmitted infections (STIs) are curable and all are treatable. But if left untreated, STIs can have long-term effects on your health. Chlamydia, for example, often has no symptoms but can affect fertility.	Every 12 months, and also at the start of a new relationship, if you've had unsafe sex or if you suspect you have an STI, if you or your partners have multiple partners and if you're planning pregnancy.
Blood pressure	The higher your blood pressure is, the higher the strain on your arteries and heart. High blood pressure damages your heart and arteries over time.	At least every two years.
Eye check	To check the health of your eyes and how well you can see.	Every two years, and more often if you have certain medical conditions (like diabetes or high blood pressure), or an eye condition.
Dental check	The health of your mouth can affect the rest of your body, and show problems with your overall health. Dental check-ups maintain the health of your teeth and gums with cleaning and fluoride, and spot potential problems early. These problems could be tooth decay, gum disease, mouth cancer or broken fillings.	Every 6–12 months, but check with your own dentist.

Health check	Why	How often
Testicular cancer (men)	Testicular cancer is rare, but it is one of the most common cancers in young men (aged between 15 and 45 years). It is also one of the most curable cancers if found early.	If you see or feel any changes, see your GP.
Cervical cancer (women)	Since the national screening program was introduced in Australia in 1991, rates of cervical cancer have halved. When it is detected early, most women are cured.	With the current cervical screening test (which replaced the pap test), women aged 25–74 should be tested every five years. (You may need other tests if you HPV test is positive.)
Breast awareness (women)	Every woman's breasts are different. What matters is anything that seems unusual to you — not just lumps, but also changes in size and shape, and any pain, dimpling, swelling or skin changes. Most of these changes are not signs of breast cancer, and cancer is rare in young women. But being aware of changes so you can see a doctor is important.	Regularly. See your doctor without delay if you notice changes.

In your 30s: Body aware

Health check	Why	How often
Skin check	To pick up skin cancers early so they can be treated and cured. Melanoma is the third most common cancer diagnosed in Australia. Melanoma is more commonly diagnosed in men than women.	Do a self-check every three months. If anything looks unusual, see your GP. In addition, see your GP for an annual skin check (or more often if needed).
Manage nutrition & alcohol consumption	Having a dietitian review your usual eating habits can make sure you're eating to fuel your health and performance, as well as catering to your unique needs.	If your health or usual dietary habits change (e.g. if you are diagnosed with coeliac disease or decide to lose weight).
Vaccinations	HPV: The HPV vaccine prevents the specific types of HPV that cause almost all cervical cancers. Flu: The flu is not a cold. Every year it causes hospitalisation and even death; in 2017, there were 1,255 deaths caused by flu in Australia. Travel: When you travel overseas you may be exposed to diseases that are preventable with immunisation.	The HPV vaccine is licensed for males aged 9–26 years and females aged 9–45 years. Women who did not have the HPV vaccine as a teenager can get it now. It involves two injections, 6–12 months apart. The flu vaccine is updated each year to protect against the strains most likely to be circulating in the coming flu season. Before you travel overseas, check with your doctor if you're due for any vaccinations.

Health check	Why	How often
Sexual health check	Most sexually transmitted infections (STIs) are curable and all are treatable. But if left untreated, STIs can have long-term effects on your health.	Every 12 months, and also at the start of a new relationship, if you've had unsafe sex or if you suspect you have an STI, if you or your partners have multiple partners and if you're planning pregnancy.
Blood pressure	The higher your blood pressure is, the higher the strain on your arteries and heart. High blood pressure damages your heart and arteries over time.	Every 2 years.
Eye check	To check the health of your eyes and how well you can see.	More often if you have certain medical conditions (like diabetes or high blood pressure), or an eye condition.
Dental check	The health of your mouth can affect the rest of your body and show problems with your overall health. Dental check-ups maintain the health of your teeth and gums with cleaning and fluoride, and spot potential problems early. These problems could be tooth decay, gum disease, mouth cancer or broken fillings.	Every 6–12 months, but check with your own dentist.

Health check	Why	How often
Testicular cancer (men)	Testicular cancer is rare, but it is one of the most common cancers in men aged between 15 and 45 years. It is also one of the most curable cancers if found early.	If you see or feel any changes, see your GP.
Cervical cancer (women)	Cervical cancer tends to occur during the 30s and 40s. It is most frequently diagnosed in women between age 35–44. Since the national screening program was introduced in Australia in 1991, rates of cervical cancer have halved. When it is detected early, most women are cured.	With the current cervical screening test (which replaced the pap test), women aged 25–74 should be tested every five years. (You may need other tests if you HPV test is positive.)
Breast awareness (women)	Every woman's breasts are different. What matters is anything that seems unusual to you — not just lumps, but also changes in size and shape, and any pain, dimpling, swelling or skin changes. Most of these changes are not signs of breast cancer, and cancer is rare in young women. But being aware of changes so you can see a doctor is important.	Regularly. See your doctor without delay if you notice changes.

Health check	Why	How often
Mindfulness and work–life integration	At this stage of life, balancing work, life and family demands can take their toll.	Talk to your GP, psychologist or executive coach during major transitions (like a new job or birth of a child) or when you need support for your mental health.
Pregnancy & family planning	To support their fertility and a healthy pregnancy and baby, both men and women need to consider their overall health, their diet, and their use of alcohol, other drugs and medications.	Before conception and during pregnancy.

In your 40s: Mindful

Health check	Why	How often
Skin check	To pick up skin cancers early so they can be treated and cured. Melanoma is the third most common cancer diagnosed in Australia. Melanoma is more commonly diagnosed in men than women.	Do a self-check every three months. If anything looks unusual, see your GP. In addition, see your GP for an annual skin check (or more often if needed).
Manage nutrition & alcohol consumption	Having a dietitian review your usual eating habits can make sure you're eating to fuel your health and performance, as well as catering to your unique needs.	If your health or usual dietary habits change (e.g. if you are diagnosed with coeliac disease, or decide to lose weight).

Health check	Why	How often
Vaccinations	Flu: The flu is not a cold. Every year it causes hospitalisation and even death; in 2017, there were 1,255 deaths caused by flu in Australia. Travel: When you travel overseas you may be exposed to diseases that are preventable with immunisation.	The flu vaccine is updated each year to protect against the strains most likely to be circulating in the coming flu season. Before you travel overseas, check with your doctor if you're due for any vaccinations.
Sexual health check	Most sexually transmitted infections (STIs) are curable and all are treatable. But if left untreated, STIs can have long-term effects on your health. Chlamydia, for example, often has no symptoms but can affect fertility.	Every 12 months, and also at the start of a new relationship, if you've had unsafe sex or if you suspect you have an STI, if you or your partners have multiple partners and if you're planning pregnancy.
Blood pressure	The higher your blood pressure is, the higher the strain on your arteries and heart. High blood pressure damages your heart and arteries over time.	At least every two years
Eye check	To check the health of your eyes and how well you can see.	Every two years. More often if you have certain medical conditions (like diabetes or high blood pressure), or an eye condition.

Health check	Why	How often
Dental check	The health of your mouth can affect the rest of your body and show problems with your overall health. Dental check-ups maintain the health of your teeth and gums with cleaning and fluoride, and spot potential problems early. These problems could be tooth decay, gum disease, mouth cancer or broken fillings.	Every 6–12 months, but check with your own dentist.
Testicular cancer (men)	Testicular cancer is rare, but it is one of the most common cancers in men aged between 15–45 years. It is also one of the most curable cancers if found early.	If you see or feel any changes, see your GP.
Cervical cancer (women)	Cervical cancer tends to occur during the 30s and 40s. It is most frequently diagnosed in women between age 35 and 44. Since the national screening program was introduced in Australia in 1991, rates of cervical cancer have halved. When it is detected early, most women are cured.	With the current cervical screening test (which replaced the pap test), women aged 25–74 should be tested every five years. (You may need other tests if you HPV test is positive.)

Health check	Why	How often
Breast awareness (women)	Rates of breast cancer begin to increase after age 40 and are highest in women over age 70.

Every woman's breasts are different. What matters is anything that seems unusual to you — not just lumps, but also changes in size and shape, and any pain, dimpling, swelling or skin changes.

Most of these changes are not signs of breast cancer but being aware of changes so you can see a doctor is important. | Conduct self-checks regularly. See your doctor without delay if you notice changes. |
| Mindfulness and work–life integration | At this stage of life, balancing work, life and family demands continues to take its toll. You may also be caring for older relatives. | Talk to your GP, psychologist or executive coach during major transitions (like a new job, or relationship breakdown) or when you need support for your mental health. |
| Cholesterol | High levels of cholesterol can mean you have a higher risk of heart disease and would benefit from making changes to your diet and lifestyle, or medication. | Cholesterol tests are usually recommended every 5 years after age 45, or earlier if you have high blood pressure or diabetes. |

Health check	Why	How often
Maintain healthy weight	In their 40s, around 4 in 10 Australians are overweight, and another 3 in 10 are obese. Carrying excess weight can make you tired and more lethargic and increases your risk of many serious and uncomfortable health conditions.	Ask your doctor to check your Body Mass Index and waist circumference every two years. You can check them yourself every few months.

In your 50s: Danger zone

Health check	Why	How often
Skin check	To pick up skin cancers early so they can be treated and cured. Melanoma is the third most common cancer diagnosed in Australia. Melanoma is more commonly diagnosed in men than women.	Do a self-check every three months. If anything looks unusual, see your GP. In addition, see your GP for an annual skin check (or more often if needed.)
Manage nutrition & alcohol consumption	Having a dietitian review your usual eating habits can make sure you're eating to fuel your health and performance, as well as catering to your unique needs.	If your health or usual dietary habits change (e.g. if you are diagnosed with coeliac disease, or decide to lose weight).

Health check	Why	How often
Vaccinations	Flu: The flu is not a cold. Every year it causes hospitalisation and even death; in 2017, there were 1,255 deaths caused by flu in Australia. Travel: When you travel overseas you may be exposed to diseases that are preventable with immunisation. Newborn grandchildren: whooping cough vaccination can protect your grandchild.	The flu vaccine is updated each year to protect against the strains most likely to be circulating in the coming flu season. Before you travel overseas, check with your doctor if you're due for any vaccinations. If you're expecting the birth of a grandchild, you should have a whooping cough booster now.
Sexual health check	Most sexually transmitted infections (STIs) are curable and all are treatable. But if left untreated, STIs can have long-term effects on your health. Chlamydia, for example, often has no symptoms but can affect fertility.	Every 12 months, and also at the start of a new relationship, if you've had unsafe sex or if you suspect you have an STI, if you or your partners have multiple partners and if you're planning pregnancy.
Blood pressure	The higher your blood pressure is, the higher the strain on your arteries and heart. High blood pressure damages your heart and arteries over time.	At least every two years
Eye check	To check the health of your eyes and how well you can see. Your lenses continue to harden as you age, so you might need to update your glasses or contacts prescription more frequently to keep up.	Every two years. More often if you have certain medical conditions (like diabetes or high blood pressure), or an eye condition.

Health check	Why	How often
Dental check	The health of your mouth can affect the rest of your body and show problems with your overall health. Dental check-ups maintain the health of your teeth and gums with cleaning and fluoride, and spot potential problems early. These problems could be tooth decay, gum disease, mouth cancer or broken fillings.	Every 6–12 months but check with your own dentist.
Cervical cancer (women)	Since the national screening program was introduced in Australia in 1991, rates of cervical cancer have halved. When it is detected early, most women are cured.	With the current cervical screening test (which replaced the pap test), women aged 25–74 should be tested every five years. (You may need other tests if you HPV test is positive.)
Breast awareness (women)	Rates of breast cancer begin to increase after age 40 and are highest in women over age 70. Every woman's breasts are different. What matters is anything that seems unusual to you — not just lumps, but also changes in size and shape, and any pain, dimpling, swelling or skin changes. Most of these changes are not signs of breast cancer but being aware of changes so you can see a doctor is important.	Conduct self-checks regularly. See your doctor without delay if you notice changes. Breastscreen encourages women over age 50 to have a free mammogram every two years.

Health check	Why	How often
Mindfulness and work-life integration	In your 50s you may be using your accumulated experience to transition to a new role or new ways of working. You may also be caring for older relatives.	Talk to your GP, psychologist or executive coach during major transitions (like a new job, children leaving home or change to part-time work) or when you need support for your mental health.
Cholesterol	High levels of cholesterol can mean you have a higher risk of heart disease, and would benefit from making changes to your diet and lifestyle, or medication.	Cholesterol tests are usually recommended every five years after age 45, or earlier if you have high blood pressure or diabetes.
Diabetes	If you're over age 45 and overweight or have high blood pressure, you're at a higher risk of developing Type-2 diabetes. Complications include heart attack, stroke, vision problems and foot ulcers.	Every three years from age 40, you should be screened using the AUSDRISK questionnaire. (Aboriginal or Torres Strait Islander people should be screened from age 18).
Maintain healthy weight	In their 40s, around 4 in 10 Australians are overweight, and another 3 in 10 are obese. Carrying excess weight can make you tired and more lethargic and increases your risk of many serious and uncomfortable health conditions.	Ask your doctor to check your Body Mass Index and waist circumference every two years. You can check them yourself every few months.

Health check	Why	How often
Hearing check	One in 3 people over the age of 50 have hearing loss, and they are often the last to know they have it. This number rises to 1 in 2 over age of 60. Hearing loss leads to fatigue, and difficulty in social and professional situations.	Every 12 months. You can check your own hearing online in ten minutes using the Blamey Saunders Speech Perception Test.
Maintain bone mass	Perimenopause causes mineral loss from women's bones. As they age, men's bone density is also affected by a decline in hormones. Risk factors include having a family history of osteoporosis, having easily broken bones, long term use of steroids, coeliac disease, overactive thyroid, and others.	Women and men over 50 with particular risk factors should talk to their doctor about a bone density scan.
Prostate exam	It is common for men over 50 to experience changes in urination, usually caused by non-cancerous enlargement of the prostate. However, prostate cancer is also a concern, causing the second highest number of cancer deaths in men (after lung cancer).	Men with concerns should speak with their doctor about any tests that may be needed. There is insufficient evidence for population-wide screening using the prostate specific antigen blood test.

Health check	Why	How often
Cardiovascular health	Cardiovascular disease (CVD) includes all diseases and conditions involving the heart and blood vessels. On average, 1 Australian dies every 12 minutes from CVD. It can also reduce your vitality and quality of life. More than four in five (83%) cardiovascular disease hospitalisations occurred in those aged 55 years and over.	Blood pressure, weight, and cholesterol checks (see previous page).
Bowel cancer	Bowel cancer is the second most common cancer in both men and women in Australia. It's more common in people over 50.	Everyone aged 50–74 should take a non-invasive test for blood in the faeces. It is offered free approximately every two years. Your doctor may also recommend other tests.

How Vicki saved her health

Vicki, aged 42, had a routine appointment with her GP for a skin check. She never missed a skin check after her brother recently had a melanoma removed. Her skin check was all clear, but her GP offered Vicki a broader health check-up while she was there.

In talking about how she was feeling, Vicki admitted to feeling particularly run down over the last several months. She often experienced her heart racing and feeling 'wound up'. It was hard to get enough rest due to the worries that went around in her mind in the night. Plus, she frequently travelled for work as Communications Manager for a nation-wide not-for-profit. Her job had become a lot more stressful lately with an organisational restructure. She often experienced headaches. Her doctor was also concerned about her blood pressure.

Vicki and her doctor agreed that, in her particular case, stress and anxiety were most likely the major contributor to her insomnia, high blood pressure and headaches. One part of her doctor's suggested treatment was developing a Mental Health Care Plan so Vicki could access funded sessions with a psychologist. It was something Vicki would never have considered unless she hit rock bottom, so she was grateful the skin check had brought her in to see the doctor. Wanting to improve her mental health also spurred Vicki to reinvest in her exercise routine and nutritional habits.

CONCLUSION

We're now faced with rapid change, technology that keeps us in constant connection with work pressures, and growing tensions between work and family responsibilities. In this current climate, many of us are finding work-life balance impossible to achieve and to keep hold of. Increasing our work–life agility is a more relevant goal.

Work–life agility lets us quickly shift our energies from one thing to another, bringing our full focus with us, and then recharging our energy to continue performing. It lets us achieve whatever is most important to us at work and at home.

Now you have a toolkit of evidence-based strategies and practical tips to improve your work-life agility. Using just a few of these will help you perform to your true potential, and simultaneously improve your wellbeing and quality of life.

There's a lot of potential actions you could take right now. I understand if you feel overwhelmed. Remember that whenever you're feeling stuck or lost, the answer is to move. Take action. No matter how small it is, get going. You start to break the inertia and build momentum toward greater vitality.

Please don't try to go it alone. You have enough on your plate already. Talk to your friends and family about your goals and get advice specific to your circumstances from health professionals.

A professional coach who has supported others in your shoes can be a tremendous asset. We can cut down the time it takes you or your organisation to implement the approach that best suits your situation. We also provide accountability and ongoing guidance.

I would love to hear from you about the challenges you face in your career, health and life, and discuss how I can help you overcome them. My contact details are in the following pages.

Good luck!

ACKNOWLEDGEMENTS

I would like to extend my sincere thanks and appreciation to the following people and organisations for their support, talents, and contribution – direct or indirect – to *Work-Life Agility*.

My family Ulrika, Diesel and Lucas thank you for your patience and encouragement, and for inspiring me to continue improving my own work-life agility.

Louise Wedgwood for all your great work over the years and helping to bring this book to life (www.wellnessinwords.com.au)

Dent Global and their Key Person Of Influence (KPI) program.

Thank you to my past and present Australian Defence Force brothers and sisters for all our shared experiences that helped shape this book. Thank you to my current and past clients for trusting me to help them achieve work-life agility. To protect their privacy, all names and identifying details of clients discussed in this book have been changed.

I would like to thank Ann Wilson and her fantastic team at Indie Experts for all their support and guidance in publishing this book. You made the whole process effortless. Thank you.

THE AUTHOR

Johnathon Herrington is a Brisbane-based performance and work–life agility coach. He helps senior executives and their teams achieve sustainable high performance and increase their vitality and capacity to flourish in complex environments. To achieve his clients' goals, Johnathon provides:

- the custom design, implementation and tracking of work–life agility strategies
- tailored performance acceleration programs
- workshops and coaching to improve executive team performance
- individual goal setting and development planning.

Johnathon comes from a high-performance background himself. In the military, he served in an elite unit. After completion of his military service, Johnathon gained formal qualifications in health and fitness, coaching and leadership and team development. He has since built a wealth of expertise with 20 years of coaching experience.

Johnathon brings a wealth of capability in performance and wellbeing coaching, having worked with a diverse range of individuals, entrepreneurs, and organisations of all sizes.

When he's not helping people grow and succeed, you can find him on the sidelines of a soccer field cheering on his two sons.

Johnathon invites you to contact him today to open a conversation about how he can help you or your organisation reach new levels of performance and purpose.

Email: hello@f3-performance.com.au
Web: http://f3-performance.com.au
LinkedIn: linkedin.com/in/johnathon-herrington

It is important to me that we support the mental health of our past and present members of the Australian Defence Force. As part of my social responsibility, I pledge to donate 10% from the profits of every book sale to a charity called Wounded Heroes Australia doing this vital work.

You can find out more information about Wounded Heroes Australia at https://www.woundedheroes.org.au

DISCLAIMER

I have made every effort to provide quality information in this book. However, I do not provide any guarantees, and assume no legal liability or responsibility for the accuracy, currency or completeness of the information.

You should obtain advice relevant to your particular circumstances from a health professional.

www.ingramcontent.com/pod-product-compliance
Lightning Source LLC
Chambersburg PA
CBHW070306010526
44107CB00056B/2505